Winning at Work

Winning
at Work

Breaking Free of Personal Traps
to Find Success in the New Workplace

Mel Sandler and Muriel Gray

Davies-Black Publishing
Palo Alto, California

Published by Davies-Black Publishing, an imprint of Consulting Psychologists Press, Inc., 3803 East Bayshore Road, Palo Alto, CA 94303; 800-624-1765.

Special discounts on bulk quantities of Davies-Black books are available to corporations, professional associations, and other organizations. For details, contact the Director of Book Sales at Davies-Black Publishing, an imprint of Consulting Psychologists Press, Inc., 3803 East Bayshore Road, Palo Alto, CA 94303; 650-691-9123; Fax 650-988-0673.

03 02 01 00 99   10 9 8 7 6 5 4 3 2 1
Printed in the United States of America

Library of Congress Cataloging-in-Publication Data

Sandler, Mel.
    Winning at work: breaking free of personal traps to find success in the new workplace / Mel Sandler, Muriel Gray.
      p. cm.
    Includes bibliographical references and index.
    ISBN 0-89106-129-0
    1. Job stress. 2. Employees—Attitudes. 3. Self-management (Psychology) I. Gray, Muriel C. II. Title.
    HF5548.85.S26   1999
    650.1—dc21   98-45306
                                            CIP
                                           Rev.

FIRST EDITION
First Printing 1999

To my wife, Leni, and my sons, Adam and Jon,
my favorite and most effective trap breakers.
—Mel Sandler

To my husband, Jack Braxton, Jr.,
who retired from the old world of work
and is courageously working at
winning in the new world.
—Muriel Gray

Contents

Preface

As professional workplace consultants, we have been involved with literally thousands of individuals who were struggling to adapt to a changing workplace. Their workplaces included large and small companies, labor unions, and government and non-profit agencies. Our work as employee assistance professionals gave us an insider's viewpoint. We consulted with people from different companies and industries in the private and public sectors, whose positions ranged from clerk to chairman and everything in between.

During the "green times"—when companies were prosperous—we listened to employees talk about having a job as security for life. They also spoke fondly of a management that showed it cared about them and listened to their concerns. When workers had job problems, they would be retrained or reassigned. If health insurance was not adequate to care for a sick family member, a manager or vice president would make sure the bill got paid.

We were also present during the arrival of the "lean times." Suddenly, these same individuals were laid off in massive numbers. We witnessed the "survivors" who attempted to cope with changing demands, as well as the managers who pushed for more work in less time. "Thank you" was replaced with "Do more" as the manager's mantra. Managers who rose to their positions during the green times, mainly because they cared and were good at motivating others, now had to heartlessly hand out layoff notices and make new demands.

We noticed that many previously successful people were now unable to cope. These were bright and talented people who suddenly became ineffective, despite their knowledge and skills. At the same time, some people who were not the best and the brightest were now thriving in this new environment. They were not necessarily the most loyal and might not have agreed with the company's position or its ways of doing things, but they were succeeding. This observation raised an obvious question: What accounted for their success?

Through our experience, we made a major discovery. People who succeeded in this new work environment had certain qualities in common—certain attitudes, personal styles, and behavioral responses. Furthermore, the individuals themselves often were not aware of many of these attitudes and behaviors. At the same time, we identified the "traps" that many people fell into. Whereas many of these personal traps were operating and tolerated prior to the organizational changes, following the changes they became magnified and perceived by others as "a problem." The workplace had become less tolerant and less forgiving of certain attitudes and behaviors. Employees who fell into one of these traps found it almost impossible to succeed in this new work environment. They became unable to use previously effective talents and people skills.

This book presents methods we have used to help people free themselves from their traps and succeed under the most difficult of circumstances. These methods have been tested in a variety of work situations. As trained consultants and psychotherapists, we have come to believe in the adage "different strokes for different folks." Our findings can be used in all work settings. We suggest that you consider what we tell you carefully and then decide which methods apply to you.

We do not claim this is an easy process—you will need to put forth effort. We will provide ideas that will apply to you, as well as to your co-workers. We ask that you use your own work situations and practice the "trap-breaking" exercises presented in this book. If you do this, you will get positive results. To gain even more insight, we ask you to identify those traps that do not apply to you but that probably apply to others around you. That way, you will increase your effectiveness in dealing with your co-workers.

In the first part of this book, we give you a general overview of the new workplace and its traps. We identify and help you resolve your major obstacles to achieving success in today's workplace—your personal traps. You will get specific solutions for how to manage each of them. In the second part of the book, we present additional strategies that we have found to be effective in dealing with traps, day-to-day work problems, and other aspects of your work life. We teach you how to incorporate these secrets of success into your work life in general.

You will meet many people whose personal and work styles and personality traits were assets in the old workplace but became major obstacles in the new workplace. You will meet managers whose attempts to implement management's new workplace changes put them in a no-win situation. You will also meet people who found themselves alienated from their families and friends as the stress of the new workplace increased, and others who were given all kinds of advice by friends and family that led them to make bad decisions. Everyone can relate to some of the personal traps described in this book. We will help you break out of these traps and write new scripts for your work life by showing you positive strategies for taking control of your career again. We cover a lot of situations, emotions, and solutions. We hope that somewhere in this mix you will find pieces of yourself or pieces of someone close to you. Let us help you find success in these turbulent times.

—Mel Sandler and Muriel Gray

Acknowledgments

We would like to acknowledge Marci Heidish and Peter Dolan, who showered us with emotional support and encouragement as they taught us about the publishing process and shared so much of their professional expertise.

—Mel Sandler and Muriel Gray

I would like to acknowledge Marty Asher, Leni Sandler, and Irwin Sandler for their guidance, support, and encouragement.

—Mel Sandler

Smaller — consultant, personal

Gray — progressive, director

(both invested in current
workplace systems, feel
use of is to adapt, adapt—
why not rebuild a workplace
system that's just,
comprehensible &
sustainable?)

Chapter 1

The New Workplace and Its Personal Traps

We seldom hear our clients complain about not having the train-ing, skill, or basic knowledge they need to do their job. Actually, we hear just the opposite. Many of the clients we see are more than qualified. They are fast learners who know how to learn the skills they need to get up to speed. Most have jobs that interest them and fit with their career goals. They have spent many years preparing for and investing in their profession. All they want is to do their job effectively and get rewarded for it. Yet, now they find themselves trapped. It's not because they don't have the ability—there's something else going on.

The Old Versus the New Workplace

Individuals have always had their own ways of acting and reacting at work. It was never a big problem. Perhaps these actions were seen as annoyances and nuisances, but they were usually no big deal—even though they may have caused some occasional career

1

difficulties. However, these same actions seem to be causing more difficulty today.

We have noticed that in the past, companies were more lenient and tolerant. They were often more prosperous as well. Employees who had difficulty coping then were more likely to receive company support. Even when people's careers were negatively affected, their company probably invested resources and energy to get them the help they needed. The company might have lightened the employee's workload or retrained or reassigned the employee. The company's goal was to do whatever it could to retain the employee.

The rules were different then. Former Secretary of Labor Robert Reich says that "companies twenty years ago or even ten years ago subscribed to a kind of implicit social contract that if a company did better, workers could be assured a reasonable degree of job security and increasing wages and benefits." The old workplace provided a clear career path that one could follow and get the rewards and promotions.

Then the rules of the workplace changed radically. Lack of predictability and rapid change became the norm. Because of this, we have found that many workers who were successful and effective in the old workplace are now having difficulty for the first time. Beverly Goldberg (1998), writing for the American Management Association's journal, *Human Resources,* sums it up like this:

> In the 1980s we were all astonished by the speed of change in the way business was conducted. We learned to run just to stay in place, and to push our organizations and ourselves to what we thought were the limits. Businesses turned to downsizing, mergers, acquisitions, teaming, quality learning, and flexibility—and put new technologies in place.

There is a great deal of pressure on workers today. The demand is that they adapt to these ever-changing working conditions. Companies and work organizations are much less tolerant than before. When employees do not perform up to expectations, the company will more than likely put pressure on them or find a way to get rid of them. For those in management (or aspiring to be), the ability to tolerate hard times is also tested. According to Greenberg (1998), surveys have found that the survival of managers has been greatly reduced in today's workplace. This is an environment that creates stress and pushes people's buttons.

The new workplace is also putting more job demands on employees. A study by Thorndike Deland Associates (cited in Kleinman, 1998) shows that many more companies are requiring that employees have crossover skills and share responsibilities. The ideal worker is one who can do more with less support. This is certainly not an environment conducive to tolerance.

Personal Attitudes in the Workplace

The following are examples of personal attitudes in the workplace. Do you see anyone you know, perhaps even yourself?

"I'M NO LONGER SPECIAL"

Barbara was a star reservations agent for a major travel agency. She was a top moneymaker. She was often excused from her position to take special familiarity tours on behalf of the agency—a form of recognition that was very important to her. Then things changed. Suddenly the company was not so good to her any more. There was no time for special training programs, and her special assignments ended. She was no longer recognized as "special." This was a significant personal blow for her. She was "just another agent." Barbara's self-esteem was affected, and her performance declined. She could no longer give her all. Her attitude got so bad that she was not even considered for a supervisory position that opened up. This further angered and hurt her and caused her to feel less appreciated, continuing the downward spiral.

"I WON'T LET THIS HAPPEN AGAIN"

Charles was an extremely hardworking plant manager. When the company took an unexpected downturn, Charles's boss informed him that there would be some drastic operational changes. His boss became very tough and demanding. Suddenly it seemed as if Charles could do nothing right. He had always prided himself on his superior work and his ability to do the right thing no matter how long it took him. Now he was being told that he didn't measure up. Charles was frightened and hurt. He was determined not to let this happen again, and began withdrawing from his work in order to "protect himself."

"I'VE PUT SO MUCH INTO THIS COMPANY"

When Ana got the assignment as proofreader she quickly learned that she had the skill to do the job. Her editor was hard to get along with but she learned how to do it. It was a sad day when the magazine was sold to a large company. Her manager kept warning Ana that her position was in jeopardy. The magazine was trying to increase its circulation by creating a new look. The old staff was going to be turned over if staff members couldn't quickly show some major creativity. In order to save her job, Ana's manager offered to reassign her to another magazine in the chain. She interpreted this as a lack of appreciation of her work and her talent and became upset. She decided to stay and make it work. For her, this was a matter of pride. The magazine was a reflection of her efforts and would continue to be so. Two months later she was looking for another job.

"I'LL SHOW THEM THEY CAN'T BEAT ME"

Ari worked hard. He reached the point of being promised a promotion. Then came some cutbacks. The number of managers was dramatically reduced, and promotions were frozen. None of the old promises counted anymore. But Ari was not the type to give up. He did everything he could to prove that he deserved this promotion. He took every opportunity to show up his current manager, whom he considered "less deserving" than he. However, his manager was in charge, and he was going to make sure that it stayed that way. He gave Ari more and more difficult assignments. None of them offered him the exposure he needed to prove himself. This only increased Ari's anger and the pace of his work. Unfortunately, each of his efforts only led to more pressure and fewer opportunities. Ari's spiral ended when he developed a stress-related ulcer and high blood pressure, which required him to take off much sick time.

"WHY SHOULD I BOTHER?"

Daniel was a salesman for a computer company that leased hardware to large companies. He was very good at what he did and made a good living. With the addition of more competitors and the introduction of less expensive systems, the company began to lose money. The turning point for Daniel came during a sales meeting when the company announced it was cutting commissions. Daniel's first thought was how unappreciated he was. Then he considered his financial problems, since he relied on his commissions to pay bills. He felt that he had been misled into believing he could count on making a certain amount of money for his efforts. This is what motivated him to work so hard. His personal disappointment became greater with time as he became less motivated to please his customers. The real shock came when a large account that Daniel was neglecting threatened to switch to another company.

"I THOUGHT THEY CARED ABOUT ME"

Judith was a sales manager in a privately owned distribution company. She was on the way up the career ladder and had a great relationship with the owner and president of the company. She truly believed she had a personal inside track. Suddenly, in response to competition, the company underwent a significant reorganization. This manager, who had been promised a promotion to the director level, found herself reporting to a tough, newly hired director who controlled her actions and reduced her authority. Judith was sure that this was a mistake. After all, she had a personal relationship with the owner and president. When she finally had had enough, she went over her new boss's head directly to her "friend," the owner. To her surprise, the owner advised her to do as she was told. It was also clear that he valued the toughness of his new director. It became shockingly clear that the company no longer had a personal commitment to Judith.

"I NO LONGER HAVE ANY FRIENDS"

Benesha was a claims adjuster in a large insurance company when the company was merged with a competitor. Benesha was thrilled to get a promotion. The tough part came when she was told about the members of her team who were not performing at acceptable levels. Suddenly she was seeing her co-worker friends in a new way. She was hearing things about them that she didn't want to know. She was also introduced to the progressive discipline that she would have to use on these "poor performers." She delivered this message seriously and let it be known that she would hold her "friends" accountable. While she was doing this she could see the distance it created and hear the whispers behind her back. She was miserable and felt that she was being disloyal and losing her best friends. She tried to be fair, but she could tell that her friends were angry with her and she was being closed out. It was clearly becoming an "us" versus "them" situation. Benesha became more and more distant from them. There wasn't even any chance that she would be asked to go with them for lunch. This rejection angered her and she started seeing these former friends as "them." She was genuinely angry.

Did you see a pattern in all of these people? Did you notice that they're all talking about how their work life has changed and about how they're having difficulty adjusting because something personal is getting in their way? All of our friends who made those statements are trapped and clearly upset about it. They are trapped by a personal attitude, which they probably don't understand, that is getting in the way of their success, Unfortunately, the consequences are often all too clear. Bringing personal attitudes into the workplace causes barriers to your career or job functioning.

In this book, we will help you identify your personal obstacles to success—your personal traps—so that you will learn how to make this new workplace work for you. We will also teach you methods, strategies, and techniques for breaking out of the traps. The examples are based on the experiences of people with whom we've actually worked. We focus on the most common situations people have presented to us. Each example is a composite of several people's situations; therefore, specific similarities between the examples and people you may know will be purely coincidental.

What are your personal traps? The following questionnaire might help you begin to identify them. Recognition and identification are the first steps toward resolving them.

Personal Traps Inventory

The following statements or thoughts are associated with the most common workplace personal traps. Does any of them apply to you?

	Yes	No
Are you bitter because of the way your company has treated you?	✓	
Is your functioning at work affected by your personal reaction to people at work?	✓	
Do you feel personally responsible for your team members?		✓
Is it hard putting in the effort when you believe that there is nothing in it for you?		
Are you frustrated when you see how selfish co-workers are unfairly rewarded?		✓
Are you stressed out because you cannot allow yourself to miss anything or make any mistakes?	✓	
When problems arise, do you expect the worst possible outcome?	✓	
Is your happiness primarily determined by how your company treats you?		✓
Do you wonder why you give your company so much of yourself?		✓
Do you worry if your manager appears upset or disapproving?		✓
Are you often angry with your manager?		✓
Are you often tense, worried, and fearful because of workplace uncertainty?	✓	
Are you experiencing stress-related physical symptoms over work-related changes?	✓	
	Yes	No

	Yes	No
Do you feel that your skills are less valued now than in the past? *b/c I dont value*	___	✓
Do you feel frustrated and find it hard to keep up with the technical and skills-related changes in your field?	✓	___
Do your family and friends complain that you have no time for them?	___	✓
Do you bring workplace tensions home with you?	___	✓
Do you resist going to others for advice?	✓	___
Do the feedback and expectations you get from friends and family about your work situation frustrate and confuse you?	___	✓
Do you believe that it's easier to do it yourself than to rely on others to do it?	___	✓
Are you frustrated as a manager because you disagree with the company's new direction?	___	___
Do you feel caught in the middle between upper management and those you directly supervise?	___	___
Are you upset because your abilities and contributions have not been recognized?	___	✓
Do you hate "tooting your own horn"?	✓	___

learned the Christian Scale / knowledge lesson too well

Each question represents one of many aspects of the personal traps discussed in this book. If you answered "Yes" to any of these questions, this book is for you because you are caught in at least one personal trap. We will help you understand and break free of them.

having somewhere often my "traps" does not resolve ? awareness in me

Common Personal Traps
and How to Manage Them

Outdated attitudes, beliefs, and expectations about the workplace can interfere with your success there. They can trap you into a work life of anger, frustration, and despair. In Part 1, we focus on the personal traps we see most frequently: taking what happens in the workplace personally, forgetting your own self-interest, having tunnel vision, being too loyal or expecting too much loyalty, and expecting co-workers to act like one big happy family. You will be encouraged to break free of them by identifying and gaining insight into your own personal traps using strategic solutions with step-by-step approaches and techniques.

Chapter 2

The "Taking It Personally" Traps

We have been impressed by the high price paid by people who take what happens in the workplace personally, particularly when the company does not accept their personal reaction. When employees fall into a "Taking It Personally" trap, they often find themselves digging deeper into a hole.

The new workplace has changed and will probably continue to change. What you need to keep in mind is that if you take it personally, you will only end up getting yourself into a trap. Remember that it's a business. You may have done well in the old workplace, but your focus is to succeed in the present. Things have changed. You need to learn to free yourself of traps you may have fallen into by taking events that are happening in the workplace personally. In this chapter, we will show you some of the common "Taking It Personally" traps and teach you some skills for breaking out of them.

Now let's revisit our friends in Chapter 1 whose personal attitudes in the workplace caused them to get caught up in so many problems and so much emotional pain that they could not imagine other ways

11

of handling their situations. They could not imagine other ways because they were locked into personalizing their situations. They were trapped into only seeing their situation one way. The key for them is to consider other possible interpretations of what was going on. Is it possible that it was not personal? Could they have misread their situations? Could they have been reacting to how they saw things rather than to what was really going on? Sometimes it seems so personal that it is difficult to consider otherwise. It is so natural for us to react to a situation the way we perceive it, but sometimes the way we see it may not be exactly the way it is. Yet, our thoughts trigger our feelings, and our feelings often trigger our behavior. This is bound to lead us to do some things that we may later regret.

A simple example might be helpful. Imagine working as a police officer and seeing a big, ferocious-looking dog running toward you. What are you thinking? What are you feeling? What will you do? We imagine you would tell yourself that you were in danger. Once you perceived this danger you would have powerful feelings of fear, anger, dread, and doom. You would act. So you would scream, run, or pull out your gun and shoot at the dog.

Now, imagine your surprise when you notice that the same dog is on a leash with a big, kind-looking owner firmly holding it. We bet you would have an entirely different reaction because you would tell yourself there was no danger. You would feel relieved and could return to being calm. Imagine what your thoughts and feelings would be if you realized that, in your panic, you had shot the poor dog.

The same pattern occurs on your job, especially when you feel that what is happening is a personal threat. Sometimes it may be personal, but often it is not. The trap comes when you can see a scenario only one way, and it is from the personal point of view. This leads to increasing stress, negative emotions, and/or regrettable action or inaction. We have observed that this trap is typically associated with specific work situations: problems with managers, times of organizational change, problems with co-workers, and problems associated with being a manager.

If you identify with any of the following "Taking It Personally" traps, this chapter will help you get out of them. We find that many successful people do not personalize at all. Even those who consider a danger as personal do not let this paralyze them. They check it out by using variations of the methods we will show you.

Personal Traps with Your Manager

The relationship between managers and the people they manage is complicated because it is a relationship with many facets. Therefore, it is easily and often misunderstood, leaving many workers and their managers misinterpreting each other's behaviors. As a result, there are many traps both can fall into.

▶ **PERSONAL TRAP**

"My manager's out to get me"

Kathryn was an architect working on a big project with a bare-bones staff. The project was over budget. Her manager would routinely come into the work area and berate the team for doing unacceptable work and not meeting their projected goal. He would usually choose one person at a time on whom to vent his anger. Everyone would have his or her turn, but nobody knew when it would come. Kathryn could hardly bear the tension and became obsessed with not making any mistake that would attract her manager's attention. She became preoccupied with the attacks and how she could avoid them.

Elliot was an art director for a popular magazine. The management decided that it needed to revamp its image and increase its readership while running an efficient operation. The managing editor was insulting to the entire team and shouted criticism freely, often in front of others. Elliot was enraged by this behavior. He just could not handle the intensity of the manager's anger and the fear and confusion that her style caused. He could only think of the insults that he endured or would endure. Elliot was so angry that he could hardly keep his mind on his work. Most of his energy went toward trying to control his temper. He feared that one day he would show his anger, regardless of the consequences.

▷ **STRATEGIC SOLUTION**   *1. Are I reacting personally?*

▷ *Shift your point of view*

In order to survive, Kathryn and Elliot had to first recognize that they were falling into the trap of reacting personally to their manager. Their response to the assaulting and threatening attacks was to think that their manager was "out to get them." This thinking would, of course, stimulate their fearful and angry emotions. These uncomfortable emotions would get in the way of their ability to function. Worse yet, it might cause them to do or say something that they would later regret.

The important thing to remember is that there are rules for the workplace that have nothing to do with one's personal life. Successful people do not allow their reactions at work to be dominated by personal attitudes. They know why they are there, and their actions are guided by what they feel to be in their best interest. Kathryn and Elliot had to remind themselves of their primary reasons for being at work. This motivation had to guide their actions. Kathryn knew that one of the main reasons she was there was to support her family and maintain their lifestyle. Elliot was there because he wanted to take advantage of opportunities to express his creativity and advance his career. Neither of them had any interest in developing a positive, primary, personal relationship with his or her manager. Yet what they wanted to get out of their work was being jeopardized because they had become trapped by their personal reactions to this very person.

Remembering and focusing on why they were there helped them to see their job situation differently. They had to be ready to work at shifting their view of what was happening to them. They had to be willing to question their personalized reactions and consider other explanations. This required that they begin by gathering information and being open to understanding things from a different perspective.

Kathryn and Elliot had to shift their point of view regarding their manager as well. They had to work on seeing him or her as a part of the workplace. They had to understand that their manager was a messenger who carried out the policies and orders handed

2. Are there other explanations (Gather info, remain open)

down to him or her. In their cases, the manager happened to convey the messages with a negative attitude and a harsh voice rather than with support and a smile. Regardless of the tone, each was delivering the same message—something was not right, and changes had to be made.

Kathryn and Elliot also had to shift to a point of view that allowed them to focus on working with their manager in order to achieve what everyone was being paid and evaluated for—doing their job. They needed to obtain as much information about doing their job and meeting expectations as possible. This information needed to come from their manager. In fact, it *was* coming from the manager, but personal reactions to their manager's style of delivery made it difficult for them to hear the message. They needed to learn to focus on the meaning and content of their manager's words rather than his or her method of delivery.

For the first time, Kathryn could hear that her manager was telling her they were under pressure. The company wanted to do things a different way. There were new expectations and new procedures. The message was that she had better change her way of doing things, too. Kathryn realized that she had to make some important changes, become a quick learner, and become proactive. She decided to schedule regular feedback meetings with her manager instead of passively waiting for angry feedback from him. She now felt more in control.

Kathryn also recognized that, despite her new level of understanding, her manager's attacks could still provoke an automatic fear response in her that got in the way of her effectiveness. She needed to learn how to control this emotional reaction.

Kathryn studied several techniques that she could use to protect herself from her fear response. She chose a visualization technique in which she imagined that an invisible shield of cellophane was surrounding her. When her manager started to verbally attack her, she visualized the anger hitting against the shield and rolling off. She could now focus on the content of what he said. (This and other useful control techniques that we have found particularly useful in the workplace are discussed in greater detail in Chapter 7.)

Understanding his managing editor as a messenger also helped Elliot focus on the message. He heard the message—they could all be in real trouble. He, too, heard that he had to start doing things differently. He also heard that his position was not secure and began to search for other options.

Like Kathryn, Elliot found that despite his understanding, he could not always control his anger response to his manager's attacks. In his case, practicing a couple of simple techniques worked. When his manager started attacking, Elliot began tightening and loosening his fist to divert his energy and help him stay calm. Afterward he started breathing slowly from his diaphragm to slow down the adrenaline, while silently telling himself to hear the words. (This method is also described in Chapter 7.) When he was able to remove himself from the point of view of hearing only a personal attack, he was surprised at what he heard.

You can also learn to effectively interact with a manager, regardless of how difficult his or her style may be. Acting with your mind rather than your emotions is critical. Focusing on the message instead of the messenger is key. If the message you hear is that you need to change the way you work (and if you want to remain there), it will be necessary to develop a strategy to make those changes. If you decide to leave, it still makes sense to use the successes on this job as a base for your next career move.

Do not forget that managers are under pressure. Just as in our example of the police officer and the dog, you may find that your manager is also on a leash—one that is held by upper management. If the managers do not see to it that the work gets done, regardless of how unreasonable, they are in jeopardy of losing their jobs. If your manager is in a pressure cooker, you and the team are under the same lid. Everyone has a manager.

▶ **PERSONAL TRAP**

"My manager let me down"

Johanna was a librarian for an insurance company, a position that entailed intense pressure and deadlines. She had a very positive relationship with her boss, who was always ready to help out in a pinch. Her boss's support, availability, and encouraging feedback, regardless of the pressure, made it all seem worthwhile.

Then came the word that the library staff were not as efficient as they should be and that they needed to respond more quickly to requests. If they didn't comply, the company threatened to contract out these services. Suddenly Johanna's boss became less available and focused all his attention on the need to work faster. Instead of approval she get questions about the speed of her work. Try as she might, she couldn't get praise even for heroic efforts. In fact, he barely greeted her in the mornings. Now going to work was torture and all Johanna could think about was the pressure of this thankless job.

She became increasingly insecure and unsure of her work, longing for the good old days when she had a connection with her boss. Without it she didn't look forward to going to work. After a while she just assumed her work was not appreciated. Why bother? She thought. I don't get recognition for my work anyway. She began to slack off and put in less effort.

Amelio was a triner for a major corporation. He loved his work and the support he received from his manager. He knew that he could always get valuable direction and feedback from her. The company was large and there were many requests for trainings. Thanks to Amelio's manager, these assignments were always framed in a very clear and doable manner. Then, in response to a changing market, the company restructured many of its procedures, resulting in fewer staff to cover assignments. The trainers were now confronting a workforce that was understaffed and that viewed attending training sessions as an unwelcome burden. They met a great deal of resistance and resentment. In addition, they got neither support nor understanding from their boss, who didn't want to hear any feedback. She just accepted the assignments as given, no longer carefully designing them, and threw the trainers into the fray. Most of her time was spent talking with and pleasing management and maintaining her position.

Amelio felt that his boss had caved in and was no longer capable of running the department adequately. This made him feel abandoned, vulnerable, and at risk for job loss. He kept thinking about how many mistakes this once-smart boss was now making.

Most of his conversations with his co-workers centered around their mutual anger at this boss who was "only watching her back" and thus messing them up. If things went wrong, they blamed their boss. They truly found the "bad guy" in this big company—their boss. Amelio couldn't see himself staying with the company very much longer and began looking into making compromise career moves just to get out of there.

▷ **STRATEGIC SOLUTION**

> *Take charge of yourself and your career*

The mistake Johanna and Amelio were making was giving away their personal power to their manager. Their feelings about their work were tied directly to their connection with and feelings about their manager. Each looked to his or her manager for motivation, approval, and confirmation of his or her competence. Johanna continually looked to her manager for messages of special connection, approval, and support. Amelio needed his manager to be a competent and effective leader in his eyes in order for him to feel a sense of safety, fairness, and purpose.

To succeed in this new environment, Johanna and Amelio had to recognize that they were confusing their personal connection with and reaction to their manager with their manager's personal style. As a result, they were giving their manager too much control and power over them. After all, Johanna's manager wasn't telling her that she was doing a bad job or that her job was at risk. She wasn't being told that she was any less competent. In fact, she was being given more responsibility and independence. And it wasn't that her manager was having a party. He was responding to his own work-related pressures. Maybe that's all he could do under the circumstances.

Amelio had no evidence that his manager was any less competent than before or that the direction she gave him was not correct. In fact, the evidence was that his group was being given much more responsibility and entrusted to be major players during the change process. Certainly this added to their value. Could it be that their manager was really redefining and trying to protect their positions? Was it possible that the manager had to learn new skills to manage this new assignment?

Johanna and Emilio's major task was to reclaim their motivation and sense of competence. They needed to evaluate their own job performance and get a sense of what they had to do in this very demanding and changing environment. They needed to see their managers for what they were: the company's messengers who were doing what they could to survive, just as they were. In other words, Johanna and Amelio needed to shift gears with confidence and recognize that they had an opportunity to work in a different way, learn something new, and even get compensated for it!

However, they also needed to take some responsibility for this "opportunity." They needed to ascertain what they had to learn in order to succeed in this environment, determine where they could learn it, and then begin to do it. They were right to want feedback, but could they get it from someone slse? Why must their manager be their only teacher and evaluator? They needed to recognize that their manager had only limited power. When changes are occurring, successful managers need to be in touch with the decision makers. They have to receive the company's changing messages and make sure that their team continues to be seen by the company as having value in the changing organization. Otherwise, they won't be there for long.

Personal Traps Involving Organizational Change

Many successful workers achieved their success while in a work environment that they knew well and in which they felt secure. Then came a downsizing, merger, or acquisition, and the organization they had known ceased to exist. They went into crisis, survival, or attack mode. They felt betrayed and interpreted a business decision as a personal attack. This kind of reaction can trap you into a counterproductive spiral of emotional behaviors. Here's how.

▶ **PERSONAL TRAP**

"They're trying to get rid of me"

Maria was a human resources specialist in a company undergoing a large-scale downsizing. From the beginning of the downsizing process, her workload increased. She wanted to do a good job and often put in fourteen-hour days in order to get the work done. Even then, it seemed as if she never got caught up. Maria had prided herself on always being able to handle the job. She was now devastated that she could not keep up. She began to work even harder and longer. The harder and longer she worked, the more frustrated, resentful, and fearful she became. She used to feel valued and supported, but now she felt betrayed and abandoned by her manager. She began to think her manager was setting her up in order to get rid of her.

▷ STRATEGIC SOLUTION

Broaden your view

Maria's situation and her reaction are typical in companies that are rapidly changing. The companies change the rules as they go along, and employees often try to second-guess them. This results in a workplace that is short on praise and long on criticism and changing demands. It also results in employees who are anxious, fearful, and questioning of their self-worth.

Like Maria, most of us often have difficulty separating who we are as people from what happens at work. Our self-worth is determined by what happens there. For many of us, the workplace is the primary place where we feel competent, appreciated, and valued. When we stop getting those positive messages from work, or when we get negative or confusing messages, we automatically start thinking it is personal. It usually isn't.

As you see with Maria, personal reactions to organizational changes are different from personal reactions to people in the workplace, such as managers. Unlike Kathryn and Elliot, Maria did not have a difficult manager to react to. She did not have a villain on whom to focus her anger or fear. This made it hard for Maria to figure out what was going on. Her mind started to play tricks on her as she attempted to figure it out. She began to imagine the worst. This personalized thinking triggered emotional reactions. Her anger, fear, and frustration distracted her from evaluating what was really going on with the company. She interpreted everything that happened as being directed at her.

The challenge for Maria was to broaden her view. That meant searching for *all* of the evidence—including that which did not support her thoughts of being set up or singled out to be fired. Maria began to do some reality checking. She talked with her coworkers about their experiences and asked for specific examples. Her purpose was to get reliable information and evaluate it objectively. In order to do this, she had to calm herself and make sure she did not come across as a complainer or someone who was feeling panic. She also did not want to fuel the suspicions of her coworkers and set the tone for negative feedback. She knew that such negativity would color her thinking. Her goal was to avoid the personal, emotionally based feedback she did not need and to get only the facts. To be certain that she was not prejudicing her conclusions, Maria asked for and received many specific examples.

Maria was surprised at what she learned. She learned that the evidence did not support her automatic response that her manager was trying to set her up in order to get rid of her. Talking with coworkers who were experiencing similar treatment from the manager made her realize she had not been singled out. Most of them were also behind in their work. She also learned that the company management was dealing with uncertainty from day to day. This trickled down to them. It was clearly a new way of doing business. Now when her work piled up she was able to see it as part of the new reality. This realization stopped her from thinking she was being set up and allowed her to do the best she could under these new circumstances.

▶ PERSONAL TRAP

"They can't do this to me"

Justine worked for a nationwide healthcare company. She had taken a position with her company because she wanted job security and mobility. Her job was very demanding and required a lot of travel. She had moved several times, but this was a sacrifice that she had been willing to make. Her work was the center of her life.

Recently her company had downsized. Her manager presented her with the bad news: Justine was being demoted and placed on a one-year special assignment. At the end of the year, if no other position had been found for her, she would be let go. She was devastated. Her first reaction was—"After all the sacrifices I've made for this company, they can't do this to me."

Justine took it very personally. She was not able to do her new job because she spent most of her time trying to figure out why the company had done this to her. When she wasn't crying and feeling depressed, she fluctuated to the other extreme—thinking that this really wasn't happening and that the company would find another position for her. Her self-esteem was at an all-time low, and she began to doubt her abilities. It became difficult for her to concentrate on day-to-day tasks, and even more difficult for her to think about the future.

▷ STRATEGIC SOLUTION

Accept reality

The challenge for Justine was to deal with her feelings of personal betrayal and to begin to understand and accept the reality of her situation. Updating her resume helped her begin to appreciate her accomplishments and recognize her marketable skills. She clearly and closely looked at the second wave of downsizing. Watching others—whom she knew to be competent—being demoted or even let go helped her realize she had not been singled out. She was also able to see the proverbial handwriting on the wall and began an aggressive external job-search campaign. Eventually, she was even able to counsel others affected by the second downsizing wave with the advice, "Don't take it personally."

Personal Traps with Your Co-Workers

Few people truly work alone. They rely on co-workers—and co-workers rely on them—to get the job done and to create the kind of workplace that makes them feel good about being there. They become very close—for better or for worse. The new workplace of layoffs and reorganizations can create tension among co-workers as they begin to see each other as competitors for dwindling numbers of positions. Those who survive a layoff or merger may experience stress and interpersonal conflicts resulting from uncertainty about their future and feelings of "survivor's guilt." Too often, they are only waiting for the other shoe to drop. Let's see.

▶ **P E R S O N A L   T R A P**

"They want my job"

Andrew was an administrative assistant in a prestigious law firm. Recently, there had been rumors that there might be a downsizing and a reduction in the support staff. Andrew, who was normally self-confident and able to read situations fairly accurately, was not too concerned. He had been at the firm longer than most of his co-workers and was well regarded by the executives he worked for.

Andrew's relationship with his co-workers had always been cordial but somewhat aloof. He did not do much socializing with them. However, he began to notice that since the reorganization rumors had arisen, the office climate had changed. Office relations seemed to be very strained and tense. His co-workers had little to say to him. He missed an important deadline and suspected that his co-workers had deliberately not told him about it. He could not help but think they wanted him to lose his job in order to save theirs.

Andrew became preoccupied with the interactions among the other co-workers. He thought he was being talked about whenever he saw them together or behind closed doors with the manager. He began to question his own judgment and abilities. He was losing sleep and became emotionally upset on the job. He missed work because whenever he would even think about the office he would feel physically ill. He did not want to confront his co-workers about what he thought he was seeing, and he considered quitting.

▷ **STRATEGIC SOLUTION**

Join the suspects

The challenge for Andrew was to talk with his co-workers about their experiences. He would have to hear what they were saying. He began to join in on conversations during breaks and at lunch. He found out that everybody was in a survival mode and that the office environment had changed to a competitive one. Everyone seemed to be preoccupied with his or her own survival. They were not out for his job, they just wanted to save their own.

As soon as Andrew recognized that the rules had changed, he decided that he either had to play by them or be left out. He recognized that he had to remain aware of what was going on and became more involved with his co-workers. He began to develop a strategy for survival. He also learned that he had to "toot his own horn." He had to learn to be competitive in his own way.

▶ **PERSONAL TRAP**

"Why them and not me?"

Elise was an accountant working in the audit department of a large investment firm. The work was hard, but she and her co-workers were a strong and cohesive team. When the company announced a downsizing plan, Elise's department was one of the targeted areas. Layoffs were supposed to be based on a set of criteria involving job performance and skills needed.

When the notices went out and Elise was not laid off, she was, at first, relieved and joyful. However, when she saw the look on the face of a co-worker who had received a layoff notice, she suddenly felt guilty. She began to question whether she deserved to keep her job. Her doubts were intensified when she had to face eight other co-workers who also had received bad news. "Why them? Why not me?" she wondered.

It was no easier for Elise after they were gone. She faced eight empty desks and other disheartened survivors. There was suddenly a lot more work with fewer employees to accomplish it. They were all feeling overwhelmed. Morale was at an all-time low in the department. To make matters worse, Elise felt guilty for doing the work that her laid-off colleagues would have been doing. She blamed herself for their fate. Her guilt got in the way of her ability to concentrate on her work. She knew that these feelings and her mood were interfering with her work.

▷ **STRATEGIC SOLUTION**

Join the survivors

The "guilt trap" is common in many people who have survived a layoff. This "survivor's guilt" often affects the morale of an entire workforce.

Unfortunately, Elise was in a lose-lose situation. She would have been devastated if she had been laid off, and she was devastated that others were let go and she wasn't. By taking responsibility for her co-workers' job loss, Elise was giving herself credit for having power that she really didn't have. She had no control over the decisions the firm made. She did not determine who would stay and who would leave. In order to overcome her survivor's guilt, Elise had to be ready to deal with her feelings of personal responsibility. In addition to trying to logically understand the situation, she needed to understand that her concern for her co-workers and her feelings of loss would naturally cause sadness.

Elise began to recover when she realized that she was probably not the only person with those feelings. Openly talking to other survivors about their loss was important. Elise and others started a support group to help employees coping with change. The group helped them grieve their loss while moving on to accept their new reality. They were able to begin to look at their crisis as an opportunity rather than a danger and to see themselves as employees with opportunities rather than as victims or guilty survivors. They also recognized that those who had been laid off shouldn't view themselves as victims. They, too, needed to see themselves as survivors who were pursuing opportunities. This would change the negative thinking that had been overtaking all of them.

Elise eventually was able to do her work without feeling guilty. She also was able to think about finding a job with another company without feeling guilty about leaving her co-workers behind.

Personal Traps When You Are the Manager

Successful managers support, motivate, and encourage their employees to be the best they can be. At times, they have to advocate or "go to bat" for them, which involves a certain degree of identification with what the employees are going through and what they need to get the job done. But as upper management's messengers, managers are also often charged with delivering harsh edicts and bad news. In trying to balance these two potentially conflicting roles, managers can easily get trapped. Here are some examples of common traps and how to manage them.

▶ PERSONAL TRAP

"I'm caught in the middle"

Elizabeth was manager of customer service agents for a large manufacturing company. Her job was to enforce demanding and strict work rules, many of which she didn't agree with herself. She was the only manager in her area, and it was her responsibility to interpret and enforce the rules. It was clear to everyone that her employees were unhappy and that they felt overwhelmed. Elizabeth also felt overburdened. She was the one who had to hear all of the complaints and deal with the resentments of an overworked workforce—particularly those she had to discipline. She got the brunt of the anger that was really meant for the company.

Elizabeth felt like she was caught in the middle between upper management and her employees. She could not stand feeling isolated and disliked. She did not want to be thought of as the bad guy. It became more difficult for her to face her team. She was easily irritated by her employees' anger and interpreted their complaints as personal attacks against her. She also became resentful of her own manager for making her into a bad guy by expecting her to heap more work on her team. She was losing her grip and aware that she was losing her temper. She realized that her reactions were going to get her into trouble, but she felt she could not control them.

▷ STRATEGIC SOLUTION

Join your club

Elizabeth decided she needed to find a different way to cope. She began by swallowing her pride and turning to her fellow managers for their ideas and support. They helped her understand her managerial role as the messenger who is delivering a very harsh message. She needed to learn that if her employees were angry they were angry at the message. She had to accept their right to be angry and frustrated.

Elizabeth was able to depersonalize her role as manager by constantly reminding herself that she did not create the message, she merely delivered it. She saw her employees' anger as a message sent to the company through her rather than as personal anger directed at her. This understanding helped Elizabeth feel much more comfortable and in control.

To help her deal with her employees' anger, she used the same technique that was helpful for Kathryn in dealing with her reaction to her manager—the imaginary shield technique—and just let the criticism roll off her back. (Chapter 7 will offer other useful techniques.)

▶ **P E R S O N A L   T R A P**

"It's all my fault"

Ben was a manager of operations in a shipping company. His job was very demanding. He had to answer to the general manager, the sales manager, and disgruntled customers. He also had to deal with the performance of his employees. He knew all of his employees on a first-name basis, felt a personal affinity toward them, and always tried to be fair. He also had met many of their families at company functions and felt a sense of responsibility toward them as well. When his employees did not perform their work in an acceptable manner, Ben would do his best to help them keep their job. He would reassign them, worry about them, or offer them light duty. He talked tough, but he was always looking out for his employees.

The company became concerned about costs and contracted with an efficiency consultant. The consultant determined that Ben's work group was labor intensive. His caretaking had resulted in having too many employees for his team's assignment. Ben's performance records were audited, and the consultant determined that he had employees whose absences and lateness were well over acceptable levels.

At the same time, a new general manager was appointed to set a new course for the company. He was tough and demanded that the workforce be cut and that employees not performing at acceptable levels be disciplined and let go. Ben was made aware that if he could not accomplish the general manager's goals, he would lose his job. Yet he felt very responsible for his people. He felt that if they got fired it was his fault. He was in a terrible predicament: He didn't want to let them down, yet his own survival was at stake.

Now that Ben's job was in jeopardy, he was shocked into rethinking what he was doing and how that fit with why he was there in the first place. He had to acknowledge that his primary reason for being there was to support his family, his lifestyle, and, ultimately, his survival. If he lost his job, it would result in real and practical suffering for those for whom he had a personal responsibility. In order to protect those things, Ben realized he had to change priorities at work and do things differently.

▷ **STRATEGIC SOLUTION**

Lead, don't carry

Ben recognized that he couldn't take personal responsibility for his employees and fulfill his managerial responsibilities at the same time. He realized he couldn't allow himself to feel guilty about employees who were not doing what they were paid to do. He had to challenge his narrow view and look at the hard facts.

Ben studied his people's job performance records and tried to figure out why they had such poor performance. He also looked to other managers for suggestions and studied what they were doing. He discovered that he was caught in a personal responsibility trap. He had protected his employees from taking responsibility for their actions. When their performance was unacceptable, he saved them rather than putting responsibility on them to improve. It became clear to Ben that he was expected to improve, and that it was not the general manager's responsibility to save him. Neither was it his responsibility to save his people. It was a workplace, not a family.

Ben had to change his idea of what a manager does. He recognized that the company was paying him to manage his people according to its expectation; he was the company's messenger. His job was to make sure that the work got done and that he directed his people to do it according to company standards. In return, the employees were responsible for doing the job that they were paid to do. For the first time, it seemed very clear to Ben—there was nothing personal in this mix. If a worker's performance was unsatisfactory, Ben recognized that he needed to address this directly. He learned some specific techniques to use when counseling employees about job performance expectations.

It wasn't easy, but Ben began to focus on his employees' job performance rather than personal matters. He identified the things that they did well, but he also identified specific performance problems. He stated clearly what was expected of them in order to show improvement, stated the consequences if things did not improve, and scheduled follow-up meetings with each person to evaluate his or her progress. If performance did not improve, Ben knew he had to impose discipline, which might also include letting some of them go. With this new understanding, Ben felt less burdened. It was not his fault. He could now focus on getting the job done.

The Price of Taking It Personally

When you take your job personally, you will respond in a personal way. While the company is making decisions that are geared toward survival and profit, you will be reeling in pain and disappointment. You and the company will literally be speaking different languages and living by different rules. The company's rules will be oriented toward change and survival, while yours will be personally motivated and, unfortunately, often pain producing. The company's emphasis will be on moving forward, yours on moving backward. This is clearly not a formula for success. Our method for establishing power and success in today's workplace requires that you let go of your personal traps first. You need to do this before taking the next step toward change. It can't be personal. Too often, it is this trap that pushes you into some of the other traps.

When coping with difficult situations in the workplace, your first step is to be able to think straight and react with your mind rather than your emotions. This is often easier said than done. We have found that the knowledge and approaches we have shared with you have helped the people we work with become successful. Using these approaches and the self-management techniques found in Chapter 7 has helped many of them handle their emotional reactions that resulted from the "Taking It Personally" traps.

The key to avoiding all of these traps is to depersonalize your thinking. It's now your turn to deal with your own situation. We hope the following "Taking It Personally" trap-breaking exercise will help you.

TRAP BREAKER

Taking It Personally

Identify a "Taking It Personally" trap that you have. Answer the following questions to help you plan your strategy for breaking out of it.

1. Describe your emotional reactions related to this trap.

2. What are your mistaken actions or reactions related to this trap?

3. What is your personal view that is affecting this situation?

4. What other explanations can you think of for your situation?

5. What evidence do you have that the situation is not personal?

[handwritten] She's been informative to her assistant & to others on the committee

6. What are the alternative explanations for the situation?

[handwritten] She's preoccupied w/ issues w/ the old bag on the committee, sees them as slow, maybe slow, out of synch

7. Now, what is your conclusion?

[handwritten] it's work, it's not personal

8. What changes do you need to make in your thinking, emotional reactions, and actions?

[handwritten, partially illegible]

9. How can you make these changes?

[handwritten, partially illegible]

[handwritten note at bottom, partially illegible] See her as in a hard [...] procedure — HT help her [...]

Chapter 3

The "Forgetting Self-Interest" Traps

The early settlers in our country often had to face changes that were very difficult, terribly painful, and often outright unfair. Just consider the farmers who had to deal with floods, landslides, volcanoes, droughts, famine, and locusts, as well as political and religious oppression. They knew that in order to succeed, they needed to focus on rebuilding and on paying attention to whatever this new world required. It often meant leaving all that they knew and loved and migrating to an unknown and perhaps hostile and dangerous place. Once they made that decision, they had to be committed to fully learning and working by the new rules. Their focus on their self-interest meant survival. The plight of these settlers could be compared with the unwanted changes many employees face today.

You may wonder if it is possible to think and act in your own self-interest and also be in sync with the company. The answer is yes. In many ways, it is probably a lot easier today than it would have been in the past. In this chapter, we will deal with some of the personal emotional reactions in the workplace that cause you to fall into the "Forgetting Self-Interest" traps.

Out-of-Control Traps

Many people feel that their careers are out of their control. Whereas in the past they could chart a course and be relatively sure of reaching their anticipated destination, now they feel that they are being swallowed up in a sea of uncertainty—going nowhere fast or going where they didn't plan to go. They get trapped by these out-of control feelings, and so does their job performance.

▶ **PERSONAL TRAP**

"I'm spinning my wheels"

Remember Judith, the sales manager from Chapter 1 with the "I Thought They Cared About Me" attitude? Unfortunately, Judith was so consumed by her thoughts about the injustice of her situation that she had no reserve energy or will to actually deal with the situation. These thoughts were so painful that they sapped all of her energy. She was spinning her wheels going nowhere (except maybe out the door) fast.

It is hard to be filled with angry, frustrating thoughts and at the same time focus your attention on doing a good job. In fact, it's hard to produce for someone if your focus is on how unfairly you are being treated. Given that the rules of work have changed, it's more important now than ever to learn the new rules. If you are filled with resentment, it will be difficult to learn or adjust to the very rules that are causing this resentment. If Judith continues to believe that treating the employees this new way is unjust and unfair, these thoughts will interfere with her ability to focus on learning the company's new policies. It will interfere with her ability to address her own self-interest. If she tells herself that she is responsible for the employees, she will have a difficult time with the changes she will have to implement—for example, putting employees through the downsizing process or increasing the pressure by implementing a more demanding sales quota. In other words, she will not be able to do her job.

And don't forget Barbara, with the "I'm No Longer Special" attitude. She was no longer recognized as the star of the reservation agents. What a personal comedown! Her pain and anger were so great that she could only think of getting even. Her strategy was to do less work. Her anger and pain became her main focus, and they consumed her emotional energy. Her negative attitudes competed with her opportunity to advance herself, despite her talent for what she did. Her personal emotional focus blurred her self-interest focus.

▷ **STRATEGIC SOLUTION**

Apply the one-focus rule

When you are spinning your wheels, we propose you try the one-focus rule: Focus on your own self-interest. As you have seen, any other personal focus will only get in your way.

Unfortunately, if Barbara and Judith go to work focused on thoughts other than learning and doing their job, this is bound to show itself. What employer wants to have someone around who is negative, working ineffectively, and showing her displeasure? Managers working under the new rules will have little energy or inclination to understand why their employees are upset and will be less likely to respond with personal concern. They are more likely to decide that these suffering souls don't fit in. They may find a way to neutralize or get rid of them by any number of methods, including setting them up to fail, overworking them, downsizing them, letting them go, or eliminating their position for a given period of time.

Barbara and Judith will have to make a choice about whether to survive or not. This will require that they challenge their old-rules way of thinking about their workplace and their job. Actually, who is to say that the old way of thinking is correct? Think about the early settlers when they encountered unfair new realities. Of course, we're not talking about discrimination and prejudice. If you believe you are being discriminated against, you should contact your state Equal Employment Opportunity Commission (EEOC).

So if we discount these and have equality, is *fairness* a requirement of the workplace? Must the workplace *take care* of its employees? Does today's workplace need to honor promises or commitments of yesterday's workplace? Is it responsible for its employees' lives?

As long as we think in terms of the old rules, we will be fooling ourselves and playing by them. It is true that we have been taught to think this way. These are the rules that we all were taught to hold dear. However, if you play a new game by old rules you don't have a chance to stay in it long.

We hear sports coaches advising players to focus on the task at hand while also learning to deal with distractions. For instance, a baseball player has to swing a bat at a small ball thrown at 80 to 100 miles per hour. He also has to deal with the jeering and insults of a hostile crowd who may be angry because he is in a slump—despite all of his heroic accomplishments of the past—or a detractor who tries to push his personal button. When he is at bat, if he thinks about any of these personal matters, he will never be able to focus on that little ball. Sports psychologists spend their time teaching athletes how to focus on the activities of the game, how to be in the moment, and how to avoid distractions. When the player focuses, the positive outcome benefits him and his team. This will also work for you. The first thing you have to do is learn to see personal focus as a distraction. This can be difficult because we have grown to view our thoughts and feelings as part of us.

▶ **PERSONAL TRAP**

"It's not fair"

Let's take a closer look at Ari, who developed the "I'll Show Them They Can't Beat Me" attitude. Ari was promised a promotion that he had worked very hard for. Let's analyze his perspective by looking at his words and his interpretation of his situation. Look especially at the words we have italicized:

> I put in all kinds of special effort and time because they *promised* me a promotion. I *deserved* this promotion. Then they *broke their word*. This was *the wrong thing to do. They gave me* an ulcer and high blood pressure. I can't just let them *get away* with this *unjust* and *unfair* treatment.

Ari had good reason to be upset and to want to get what was due him. He was also justified in being upset. After all, he believed he had been wronged.

▷ STRATEGIC SOLUTION

Don't be a victim

Clearly, most of the words Ari used to describe his situation were emotion-laden words of injustice. But they were also the words of a victim. Ari took his company's actions personally, and they began to define who he was, how he felt, and what he thought. In many ways, Ari's response created a self-fulfilling prophecy, enabling him to truly become the victim.

Ari's thinking needed to change. He could not think of himself as a victim and have his own self-interest in mind at the same time. As a victim, he was focused on what didn't happen, what should have happened, and how he had been wronged. He saw the focus and control as being outside of himself. Ari's problems increased because he was unable to shift the focus to his own self-interest. Shifting his focus would have allowed him to feel and think like the driver in the driver's seat. He would have begun to have the control.

Ari had several choices. One choice was to writhe in pain and sorrow. He could do this suffering in silence. He could also decide to continue trying new ways to help his manager see the light. Perhaps he could, with enough effort, show her the light. Maybe she could talk with other people in management or in the personnel department and convince them that he was deserving of the promotion. Ari could even challenge his manager. Chances are, his manager was representing upper management's carefully planned strategy and was committed to making the new system work. If Ari were to buck the new system, he would succeed in shining a big red spotlight on himself as someone who was a threat to the success of this plan. Others would probably see him as declaring warfare in their turf. It would be Ari against the management team and their consultants. Who do you think would win that one?

Or Ari might decide to get even. He could try and do this in all sorts of creative ways. It would be kind of like trying to get even with a shrewd general while serving in his army. Don't forget this general has all sorts of officers who are rewarded for their ability to make sure that the troops do their job. There might even be some soldiers who would see a reward in turning Ari in. Once he declared war, he would then become one of the general's enemies. If caught, he would become one of the victims.

Going back to our baseball analogy, can you imagine a player getting even because he felt he had been treated unfairly? What if he intentionally struck out, hit into a double play, or missed an easy fly ball? He might even take more drastic action and hit a sharp line drive at the manager's head. Who do you think would win that struggle?

We all have choices when it comes to our thoughts and behaviors. So did Ari. He could rethink some of what we have been saying. It just isn't personal. Justice and fairness are not the issue, and they never really were. When Ari was promised the promotion, the rules were just different. There are all sorts of management systems and personnel in place to make sure that these new rules are implemented. Ari needed to lick his wounds and find a way to carry on in a way that would serve his self-interest.

Anger Traps

Probably the most common traps we see are anger traps—employees getting mad rather than staying even. Inevitably, they get so trapped in their anger that they self-destruct, completely losing sight of their self-interest. Let's see how this works and what you can do about it.

▶ **PERSONAL TRAP**

"I'm mad and I don't care who knows it"

Tony was hired by the manager of a small accounting firm to handle part of the increased workload resulting from a merger. It soon became clear that Tony had certain weaknesses in how he approached some types of work. But he also had certain strengths that were important to the firm. When Tony's manager pointed out these weaknesses, Tony became angry and indignant and indicated that he felt he was being treated unfairly. He could not get past the idea that his strengths were not being acknowledged. Tony felt unappreciated. His openly expressed indignation and dissatisfaction began to cause him more problems and bring on negative attention. The result was more intense supervision and a reduction in assignments. Tony wanted to leave, but he could not afford to make a move yet.

▷ **STRATEGIC SOLUTION**

Poker anyone?

When you are playing against other card players, good or bad, you don't tell them anything about your hand. In fact, you may even smile and look confident when you have a bad or mediocre hand. You know that may encourage your competitor to pull back. On the other hand, you may show disgust when you have a good hand. This encourages the competitor to stay in. You will certainly work hard not to let your attitude or expression help your adversary figure out your real hand. Good adversaries know they have a better chance of winning if they read you and figure out your hand. In fact, an effective way to deal with a strong adversary is to put on a noncommittal poker face, put all your energy into your game, and read your adversary.

Tony decided to change his tune. He became cooperative and began to show interest in and gratitude for the suggestions and special attention. He diligently did whatever was asked of him, and more. Although he did not agree with the professional criticism, he accepted it. He acted as if he valued and appreciated it. He knew that he had nothing to lose in doing this. After all, it was their shop. He made it a point to show that he was using his manager's feedback to comply with how the company wanted things to be done. He wanted to make sure the firm felt it did not need to worry about him. This would give him room and time to network and look into other options. Then he would be able to make a move on his own schedule. He was also making it possible to continue with this firm if he decided that it would offer him his best opportunity. He did not burn bridges. Tony's manager saw that, with time, he was able to accept criticism and use it to improve and grow. She felt that he would continue to be a valued member of the group, and she worked to help him succeed. She began to handpick client assignments for him and work with his strengths. After about a year he was working with a solid client base and handling it effectively. To the manager's surprise, Tony submitted his resignation about a year and a half later. He had accepted a job with a larger firm.

Tony had secretly set a goal to succeed in the firm until he was ready to move on to a larger firm. He played poker. As you can see, he won the game. He gave himself time to regroup and take the red light off of him. With this he was seen as an asset, treated that way, and given the time to pursue his goal.

Doing your best is the best way to look out for your self-interest. It will give you the best chance to protect and achieve your goals. Doing your best means doing what you were trained or learned to do. It means not allowing your personal feelings to get in the way of practicing and succeeding in your trade. If you can make the choice, why not focus on doing your job and on being successful?

▶ PERSONAL TRAP

"There's nothing in it for me"

Judith was so upset about not getting the promised promotion and about how badly the employees were being treated that she reacted with anguish and disgust. Barbara was upset because she was no longer recognized as special; her sole focus and goal were getting even. Ari literally made himself sick with all his stress and anger.

Our poor friends lost all perspective on why they were going to work. It's as if their outcome didn't matter. Their future had no meaning. Because of the nature of the changes, they lost their focus on their goals. They were too busy focusing negatively on the changes. The injustice and pain were so great that their goals no longer mattered. They abandoned any idea that there could be anything in it for them in this new environment. This is equivalent to surrender. Instead, they needed to do what the company did when it decided to reorganize—reevaluate its basic goals, directions, and strategies.

▷ STRATEGIC SOLUTION

Set goals

The company has changed for Judith, Barbara, and Ari. They are reacting to what they see. They don't see a clear path for themselves in this new design. They need to free themselves from the trap and change their focus. In order to work toward their own self-interest, these three must have something to bring to the table. They need to determine what they want to get out of this new environment. They need to develop goals. Each of their companies started to meet its changing environment by developing goals and then went through a process geared toward achieving them. Employees must do this as well. They need to start focusing on a process leading toward developing and achieving *their* goals.

Setting goals means saying to themselves that they have worth. What they want or need counts and must be part of the picture. They can change their focus just as the company does. They can work toward forwarding their self-interest rather than reacting to what is dealt to them. This starts with refocusing on what their goals are now. Why are they going to their job? Let's imagine what their self-interest goals might be.

Judith's self-interest goals might include one or more of the following:

- ☑ Surviving a few more years until she can retire
- ☑ Finding a way to stay and survive
- ☑ Surviving long enough to be able to make an effective career move
- ☑ Leaving on good terms and having time to retrain or relocate

Her specific goals would depend on her years in service; her personal financial status and needs; her health, interests, and strengths; and many other personal considerations. They would also depend on the realities of her situation. Goal setting for Judith begins by considering her personal and professional needs. She is actively focusing on *her* goals and self-interests rather than reacting to injustices.

As Barbara formulates her goals, she might recognize that she has strong talents that she wants to utilize for career advancement. Her goals might be one or more of the following:

☑ Making more money
☑ Advancing her career in her current *new-rules* environment
☑ Surviving where she is while exploring and pursuing other job or training opportunities
☑ Leaving the company on good terms and pursuing other job opportunities

Let's look at the goal of leaving the company on good terms and pursuing other opportunities. This goal is very tricky at best. Searching for a job while being out of work can lessen Barbara's attractiveness in the job market and reduce her negotiating power. It may be in her self-interest to try to survive where she is while exploring and pursuing other job or training opportunities.

Ari's goals might look a little different. Given that his physical problems make it impossible for him to do his current job, he needs to set goals with this in mind. His finances, of course, would be an important factor in his goal setting. His list of possible goals might look like this:

☑ Trying to hold on to his current position while focusing on transferring elsewhere in the company
☑ Seeing if the Americans With Disabilities Act applies to his situation
☑ Looking for temporary employment elsewhere
☑ Seeking alternative employment with a company that can offer a future
☑ Getting retraining while seeking alternative full-time or part-time employment

Sometimes you may get some hints that your choices are very limited. In this case, you need to read the handwriting on the wall. For instance, you may remember our friend Ana from Chapter 1, who had the "I've Put So Much into This Company" attitude. She was getting some strong hints that no matter what she did, she would soon be let go from her company. Unfortunately, she ignored those hints and was totally unprepared for the bad news when it came. She refused to accept the idea that such a thing could happen to her, so she didn't see the signs—a classic case of denial.

Ana needed to move quickly. Her goals (had she not been in denial) would probably have included the following:

☑ Locating a parallel position in another company as an interim move

☑ Locating several part-time positions, each with parallel responsibilities, with the chance of advancing to a full-time job in one of the companies

☑ Seeking a position in a consulting company

☑ Seeking freelance positions

Of course, in her position it would be important for her to try to positively connect with her new management while pursuing the other goals.

Clearly, goal setting must include many personal considerations: current job realities and pressures, personal and financial needs, input of family members, interest, talent, training, opportunities in the field, and immediacy of need to act. It must also consider workplace realities and possibilities. It starts with a focus on self-interest.

Self-Interest Thinking

If you are to succeed on the job, your interests must parallel those of the company. They must also parallel your own vision of the future—your future. The focus must be on a better fit between you and the company. The company is adjusting in order to look out for its interests, and so must you.

We are sure you know that what you are about to do will not be easy. However, you will be empowered and gratified knowing that you are advancing your self-interest and career. You are working toward *your* goals. Furthermore, this is certainly better than being overwhelmed with anger or feeling out of control.

The following exercise will help you develop self-interest thinking.

Forgetting Self-Interests

Think about your goals. Don't focus on the company yet or on how to achieve your goals—that will come later. For now, think about what you want and what is feasible. These may be two separate things. We want you to dream and also be realistic.

Give yourself a menu of goals to work with. Let your mind go in the realm of the possible. If you have only one track, it may lead to a dead end or very rocky terrain. List several goals so that you can have a broad range of options. Limitations at this point will narrow your options in an already difficult environment.

Feasible Goals

1. *Meaningful work*
2. *40–80 % fence*
3. *w/ people*
(4. *Working treated w/ respect, compassion*)
5.
6. *volunteer my skills → and I believe*

Now make a second list of goals. This is your wish list. A wish list of goals needs to be different from your previous one, which was more doable. This list will bring you closer to what you would like in the best of circumstances. It is a way to stretch your vision. It is a way to integrate your strengths and aspirations.

For example, Barbara might wish to gain advancement and an increase in pay. Ari might wish for a supervisory position. Judith might want to do her human resources work in a different and more gratifying way. Given their current situations, those goals are not feasible. They are in the realm of the ideal, at least at this time. However, in the future such goals might be achievable with some planning, a vision, and the determination to overcome personal emotional traps.

Wish List Goals

1. Partner in small, creative,
2. Complementary effort
3. respected about what I'm doing
4. part of a real team – think, create, produce tangible
5. Engaged people
6. just do it, cut the red tape

Now let's compare and see if we can combine the two lists. Put both lists side by side and analyze them by answering the following questions:

- Are there any feasible goals that are similar to your wish list goals? If so, combine them. This will be your first goal of a third list of action goals.
- Are there any achievable wish list goals that can be achieved while working on a feasible goal? If so, enter that next on the action goals list.
- Can you make any compromises that might combine any of your feasibility and wish list goals? If so, list them next.
- If any of the remaining goals fit with any of the above matches, combine them and put it on the new list.
- Don't discard your goals. Just because they don't seem feasible now doesn't mean that they won't be in the future. They should be listed next on the action goals list.
- The same applies to your unused wish list goals. They could become feasible. You could make that happen in the future. Always keep room for this to happen. List these goals next.

Action Goals Engaged

1. Small team, partnership
2.
3.

4.

5.

6.

Now develop a plan that will set you in motion and move you toward your action goals.

Chapter 4

The "Tunnel Vision" Traps

Imagine being in a long, narrow tunnel. This is a tunnel that you've traveled often. Now imagine looking around you. What do you see? Where can you go? Chances are you can only see or go in one narrow direction either in front of or behind you. How do you feel as you look at this familiar sight? If it's familiar and predictable, we expect that you will be comfortable. Suddenly, you hear all kinds of rumbling noises beyond the firm walls of the same tunnel. Now what do you see? Where can you go? How do you feel now? You still have that same view limited by the tunnel wall. Yet you can hear that there is danger beyond the walls. The problem is that you can't see what it is, you can't get to it, and you can't get away from it.

The walls of the tunnels in the workplace are constructed of personal beliefs. Many of these personal beliefs are long held and just as firm as a solid wall. They put the same limits on your ability to view things and to move forward as a wall would. When things are familiar, this narrow view is limiting but you can adjust. When there are major rumblings of change at the workplace, your inability to see or move beyond these walls can lead to extreme fear and dangerous consequences.

There is a reason that people with tunnel vision were able to succeed in yesterday's workplace. There was a sense of order and predictability then. The companies themselves were more stable and accommodated differences. Those who could change their style and chose to stay in their company or field did so. Those who couldn't adjust left and found a company or field that was able to accommodate their style.

Our experience is that people who have tunnel vision often cannot cope in today's unstable and unpredictable workplace. In fact, because their vision is so personally limited, they often can't even see the reality as it changes, and, consequently, they do not have the information they need to act in their self-interest.

Successful people are always able to broaden their vision and see changes as they occur, and often they can even stay ahead of them. As a result they can choose to act in their self-interest as their work reality changes. In this chapter, we will show you how you can broaden your vision with some tunnel vision solutions that can convert failure to success.

Seeing-in-Black-and-White Traps

Some people see the positive in everything. We call them *optimists.* They are very confident and are sure that things will *always* work out, regardless of the reality of the situation. Sometimes it is nice to have someone like that on our work team who, regardless of the reality, will always insist on a positive view. Then there are those who always see the negative and doom in everything that happens. We call them *pessimists.* They are constant worriers and refuse to see the positive aspects of a situation. Their only vision is that the worst possibility will occur. After a while, we live with their words of doom and try to reassure them. For both optimists and pessimists, the reality of a situation has less to do with how they see their situation than with their particular type of vision.

▶ **PERSONAL TRAP**

"Everything's coming up roses"   *optimist = H*

Sunita was an account manager for a small advertising firm. No matter how bad things got, she always maintained a positive view and pushed ahead. Her doggedly positive view often gave her work team the energy to move things forward. Then her company turned upside down. A large firm acquired the agency. This firm did its best to efficiently integrate both operations. It began to put its own people in charge of many of the existing accounts. Many of Sunita's co-workers were demoted or put under rigorous controls. While many of her colleagues bailed out, Sunita continued to have an optimistic view and applied herself to her work more rigorously, trusting that it would "work out for the best." She simply could not see the negative side. Neither could she see that she was just giving the new management time to integrate her accounts into their management structure. Despite all of the negative evidence, she was shocked the day that her accounts were folded into another department and she was given the choice of taking a demotion and pay cut or a leave of absence.

Sunita's problem was that she was a tunnel vision optimist. She could only see things in positive terms. She was unable to see the peril surrounding her and, consequently, could not protect herself. It's as if she were partially blind.

Sadly for the tunnel vision optimists, they can't even consider the idea that disaster is imminent. Sunita's rose-colored glasses—her need to feel that everything was going to work out fine—filtered out the disaster that her colleagues saw coming.

▷ **STRATEGIC SOLUTION**   *The danger = and pro tect / secures*
Face the danger   *little demand to Spt.*
unity

Sunita thought that everything would be fine. She ignored the danger signals and warnings from her co-workers. Her tunnel vision resulted in her being calm and trusting. She just kept doing her job and didn't take any action to protect herself. Her thoughts were inaccurate and unfortunately produced a false sense of security. Had she thought she was in danger, she would have felt uncomfortable and tense. In this case, experiencing those uncomfortable feelings would have been a good thing because the tension might have alerted Sunita to a need to protect herself.

▶ **PERSONAL TRAP**

"It's a dangerous world out there"

Sam was a creative director for a trade magazine. He was known for being a worrier who would panic whenever the circulation was threatened or his ideas were rejected. A frown from his publisher would fill Sam with panic and doom-filled thoughts. He constantly feared that he would be fired. As a matter of fact, he referred to himself as a "dead man."

When a large magazine chain acquired Sam's magazine, people started to get laid off or reassigned. Sam became overwhelmed by the doom that actually hit. He was so anxious that he had no free energy to help him adapt to the new demands placed on him. Unfortunately, he could not even think clearly enough to develop an intelligent exit plan.

▷ STRATEGIC SOLUTION

Learn to smell the roses

Sam always thought that he was doomed, a dead man. He was often in a state of tension and fear. When it really became dangerous and his co-workers confirmed his worst fear, he thought that this time he really was dead and could do nothing about it; he was powerless to fight his fate. These feelings escalated to panic and terror, making it impossible for him to think clearly or take any kind of action. If he took action, it was irrational and had negative consequences. This is similar to our policeman friend. If he were a pessimist and saw the dog running toward him, his feelings of doom might have prevented him from viewing things clearly or noticing the leash. He might have automatically told himself that he was a dead man and protected himself by shooting the dog. The consequence would have been having to face a very irate owner of a wounded or dead dog.

For tunnel vision pessimists, life can be uncomfortable, if not intolerable. They see signs of danger everywhere and often have extreme reactions to situations that are painful and unproductive. These doomsayers need to free themselves from the spiral of negativity.

Learning to smell the roses involves developing skills that will help them learn to control their negative thoughts, their emotions, and their reaction to this self-induced stress. Some techniques for learning to do this are described in Chapter 7. The exercise at the end of this chapter is also a valuable tool.

Single-Vision Traps

Some people can't bear to have anything go wrong or be unfinished. We call them *perfectionists*. In their particular vision of the world, there is no room for anything but perfection. This view persists regardless of how difficult the task or the volume of work.

Then there are those who see work everywhere. We call them *workaholics*. Work is the only thing that has any meaning in their lives. They are trapped in a fixed way of seeing and doing and lack the flexibility to adapt to changing realities.

▶ PERSONAL TRAP

"No room for mistakes"

It is one thing for a boss or powerful person to tell us to be free from fault or defect; at least we can be angry with him or her for being so unfair and demanding, or we can try to find ways to get away with some minor mistakes. But it is another thing to constantly put this lack of tolerance for mistakes on ourselves. When we do this, we can never get away from the demand for perfection, since we must answer to someone (us) who is always looking.

Molly was manager of information systems for a large bank. She had risen to this position by being thorough and doing everything assigned to her perfectly. She simply never made any mistakes. She was known as the person to give any assignment to. She had zero tolerance for anything but perfection and always pushed to complete whatever was assigned. She was proud that she was able to achieve the impossible and did so regardless of the effort or time required. Delegating responsibility was difficult because she could never find anyone perfect enough.

Molly was able to succeed in her perfectionist style until her bank merged with another bank of comparable size. Now she was challenged to head up the effort to merge the two banks' information systems. She had a very tight timeline. She also had to take a leadership role for both banks. She believed she had to do it perfectly. She couldn't tell herself or anyone else that she couldn't handle it. Nothing could pass without her careful review. This was a superhuman task that occupied all of her time and kept her stressed out. Finally, her body succumbed to an ulcer attack. She ignored it at first—How could she allow herself to slow down long enough to be sick? she asked. In the past, Molly's tunnel vision had been rewarded by all kinds of recognition and promotions. Unfortunately, when the workplace went through a drastic change, she was not able to handle the demands.

Carlos was an inside sales rep for a large clothing manufacturer. He spent a lot of time making sure that all accounts were serviced perfectly. His great fear was that any mistake would lead to punishment and job loss. If he had even a hint that a customer was unhappy, he would immediately call and check out what he could do so he or she would be completely satisfied. He could not hang up the telephone until he was reassured by the customer's tone of voice that there was no remaining complaint. He imposed the same pressure on himself in his dealings with other sales representatives, production staff, and management. He would bend over backward to be sure that his paperwork was just right and contained no errors. If something got sent back, he experienced an overwhelming fear that compelled him to immediately fix it with an explanation. Regardless of the amount of work assigned to him, he was sure to complete all of it—with no mistakes. He was certain that failure would result in severe punishment.

When Carlos's company restructured and downsized, it also changed many of its procedures. Carlos was unable to keep up with the increased workload *and* learn all of the new procedures *and* do it all perfectly. He was also working with new people and didn't yet know what pleased them or how to read them. He became overwhelmed with the terror of being judged and fired for every "imperfect" thing that he did. This dread got in the way of his ability to think clearly and concentrate on his work. This led to increasing mistakes and clumsy interactions with co-workers. He was unable to focus on his work and started to express some of his fear through a generally negative and sarcastic attitude.

Meghan always did a perfect job. Her great dread underneath it all was that people might find out she wasn't as smart or as competent as they thought. She feared that any mistake would reveal this. She considered herself a fraud. She was a closet incompetent. As long as she didn't make any mistakes, no one would discover her terrible secret. As a trainer, she worked as long as necessary to master whatever content she had to cover. She was also constantly perfecting her style of delivery. She practiced all the time and had been a member of Toastmasters International for many years. No one must ever suspect her secret. Regardless of the effort required, she was always available to whatever department needed training.

In response to the changing market, Meghan's company had to revamp its product line and its marketing strategies. This required that the trainers play a major role in staff development. As you can imagine, this was overwhelming for Meghan. She simply couldn't avoid making mistakes. Her nightmare came true. Through her imperfect performance, she believed that people found out she was "incompetent" and a "fraud." This led to feelings of panic, shame, disgrace, and uncertainty. She became overapologetic for her mistakes. Eventually her only avenue was to start avoiding the people who she thought saw through her. She soon left the company, thinking of herself as a great failure.

▷ **STRATEGIC SOLUTION**

Look and listen

It is likely that people with tunnel vision learned their narrow way of viewing the world from past experiences—such as school experiences, special life circumstances, or career experiences—or from people who had a strong influence on them in the past—such as family members and peers. Carlos, for example, had a family that made it clear that only A's were acceptable in school. Anything less resulted in negative judgment or punishment. His teachers also expected all A's and were openly disappointed when he got anything less. Carlos learned early that he had to do everything perfectly or risk being judged negatively, and this lesson continued to affect his view of the world, including the workplace, as he got older. He needed to challenge this view and learn another way.

Molly continued to tell herself that she had to do everything completely, on time, and perfectly—even when her workload dramatically increased with the merger of the two banks. The more impossible the workload became, the more she demanded of herself. This resulted in increased feelings of tension, anxiety, and desperation and eventually led to her body's breakdown under the pressure. Had she been able to tell herself that she could let something go, prioritize, or delegate to someone who might make a mistake, she could have maintained a pace that would have considered her body's limitations. Her thoughts drove her behavior.

Molly, Carlos, and Meghan needed to acknowledge that theirs was not the only way to see things. They needed to notice that other people have very different ways of seeing the same things that they were looking at. They needed to see that there are people who are effective and successful who have very different visions. This is true for all areas of their lives—in and out of work.

Talking with co-workers about the things that were happening at work would be a good start for our friends. Many of their co-workers would appreciate an opportunity to share their view and be listened to. Listening to what they have to say, without presenting their own point of view and thereby reinforcing it, is the goal. Hopefully, our friends will eventually begin to see that their own personal way of viewing things has many credible challengers. Acting as if it is the only way is actually choosing to follow a very narrow path.

▶ **P E R S O N A L   T R A P**

"Work is my life"

Some people view the world through a tunnel that has the work-place as its only focus. Will was such a person. He was a hospital administrator who loved his work. There was always something to do and he was there for all of it. His workday started the moment he got up and lasted until he went to bed. When he wasn't work-ing he was thinking about work. Although he had a family, he spent little time with them and less time thinking about them. Then something happened to change his world.

In response to the pressures of managed care, the hospital merged with a larger facility. Will's position was restructured, resulting in a severe reduction of his responsibilities and level of influence. Sud-denly, he had a lot of free time on his hands. Will likened the feeling to "a hole in his soul." He was a workaholic who had lost his work. For him, there was nothing else. This soon led him to withdraw into sadness and despair, and Will began to drink heavily.

As we saw, Will needed work to occupy him and keep him focused. His position in the hospital had given him that. However, the hospital merger resulted in his having less responsibility and influence. It didn't take long before he had a lot of empty moments with no work to think about. During those moments he frantically asked himself what he could do, how he could fill up the time, and what he could look forward to. He also questioned his place and his value. He was lost. He began to feel panic and confusion. He lost his identity, his sense of self, his sense of impor-tance. As a result, his moods and behavior changed drastically. He began to alternate between complaining and withdrawing from others. Unfortunately, he filled the emptiness with alcohol.

▷ **S T R A T E G I C   S O L U T I O N**

See a bigger picture

Will, like other workaholics, needed to see how people could have a personal life and still be successful. In order to do this, he needed to redefine his view of success to include a more balanced lifestyle, giving importance to other values such as family and personal health.

Talking to co-workers with a more balanced lifestyle would also help. These should be people whom he likes, respects, and considers successful. He should look for evidence that a broader view is possible.

Broadening one's vision is not easy because people tend to get very attached to their particular ways of seeing things. Changing this requires a lot of work. In addition to the general solutions for tunnel vision that are presented in this chapter, the topic of maintaining a balanced lifestyle is covered more thoroughly in Chapter 9.

Challenging Tunnel Thinking

Now that you have seen that there are alternative ways of viewing events in the workplace, you can also begin to challenge your automatic thoughts. Remember our discussion in Chapter 2 about how our feelings affect our thoughts. If the policeman thought that the big dog running toward him was about to lick him, he would have warm, friendly feelings toward the dog. He might even reach out his hands to pet or hug the dog. If he thought that the dog planned to bite him, he might feel fear and run or take out his stick for protection. Clearly, it is how we think about events that makes all the difference in how we feel and how we respond. Tunnel thinking leads to tunnel vision, which causes certain actions. If we were to put this into a picture it would look like this:

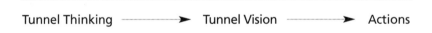

Tunnel Thinking ──────➤ Tunnel Vision ──────➤ Actions

We want you to become more familiar with your tunnel thinking and the feelings and actions that result from it. Only then can you begin to challenge it and substitute thoughts, feelings, and actions that are based on the realities around you.

Before you will be ready to take action, you need to know how to choose the correct actions. You need to wait until you have acquired the right approach and learned the best techniques. The wrong action is likely to add to your problems. The first step is to become aware of the thoughts when they come into your mind. Once you have that awareness, you can try to influence them.

We have found that people with the same type of tunnel vision often have similar thoughts. Here are some examples:

☑ A pessimist will view an event and automatically think such thoughts as these: "Oh boy, am I in trouble now"; "They'd better not find out or else …"; "I'm doomed"; or "Why do these terrible things always happen to me?"

☑ Despite the evidence and warnings, an optimist will continue to think: "Things will work out. They always do"; "I don't know why everyone is so upset; just give them a chance"; If I do what I need to, it will work out."

☑ Regardless of the work load or realistic expectations, a perfectionist will say: "I should have done that a little better"; "I can't turn it in like that"; "This will be the last change"; or "It's not quite right yet."

☑ A workaholic will say: "I eat, sleep, and dream my job"; "I have so much to do, I have no time for anything else"; or "How am I going to get all of this work done?"

Clearly, if you repeatedly tell yourself something you will believe it, whether it is true or not. That is why you need to begin to question your thoughts just as you questioned your tunnel vision. In the strategy presented here, we utilized cognitive behavioral strategies such as those described in David Burns's book *Feeling Good.*

When an automatic thought comes to mind, you need to consciously substitute an alternative one. These alternative thoughts need to be repeated often. Don't forget, you are challenging a long-held pattern of seeing and thinking.

The following chart shows some typical automatic thoughts along with some alternative thoughts that could be substituted for them.

isolated? won't always be

chart one *longer, more than opt/pess, perfect/wonderful*

Right Thinking

Tunnel Thinking	Broader Thinking
Optimist	
Things will work out. They always do.	This might not work out, no matter what I or others do.
If I do the right thing, things will work out the right way.	This is different from what I expected.
I don't know why everyone is so upset; just give them a chance.	Study what people have to say; they can't all be wrong.
Pessimist	
I'm doomed.	What is another possible outcome?
Am I in trouble now!	Is there any evidence to the contrary?
I'm dead.	Is this a false alarm?
Why do terrible things always happen to me?	Good things have happened to me. They also count.
Perfectionist	
It better all get done.	Is it all equally important?
There can't be any mistakes.	What is realistic given the circumstances?
If they see that, they will fire me.	When is the last time someone got fired for not being perfect?
If they see that, they will know I am a fraud.	Why am I a fraud for doing what my co-workers do and accept?
I must be number one.	Who is keeping score?
Workaholic	
The job has such pressure that it's always on my mind.	How does constantly thinking about the job help my performance?
I have so much to do I have no time for anything else.	If I didn't work all the time, what else would I have time for?

Now it's your turn. Make your own list. If need be, consult with your co-workers, friends, and family.

TRAP BREAKER

Tunnel Vision

Write an automatic thought, then think of an alternative thought that may also be true. Just write down a whole bunch of such thought pairs. Then, when you start to walk down your personal tunnel, substitute some of the alternative thoughts. You may also have to ask yourself questions that will help you challenge your thinking. It may feel like you're debating or arguing with yourself. You are!

Tunnel Thinking	Broader Thinking
1. *I'm a tech/science writer*	1. *I can do many things that others value*
2. *I'm a public servant*	2. *I can work many places*
3.	3. *where*
4.	4.
5.	5.
6.	6.

Remember that we are creatures of habit and don't break old patterns easily. Recognize this and accept the fact that the change process may occur in steps.

Challenge one thing that you do and try doing it another way. Start with a project that is not critical. (If you can't determine what is less and more important, you will need to develop that skill.) Then delegate the project or don't do it perfectly. Let it go, and imagine closing the book on it. Then reality check it after some time passes. See if a disaster results. If a problem arises, is it fatal? Can it be handled? Are people rejecting as a result? Take it in. Then try another project.

Your goal is not to be a sloppy worker—just to allow for the same margin of error or imperfection that others have in order to survive.

Chapter 5

The "Loyalty" Traps

Confusion about loyalty is a major reason that many people have problems in the new workplace. What many people do not recognize is that a big change has occurred regarding rules about loyalty. Effective use of loyalty is one of the primary ingredients for career success today. Ineffective use of loyalty is one of the common ways in which we get trapped. You will need to take a closer look at what exactly is meant by loyalty in the new workplace and learn to use it to your advantage in your job and career.

Most of us have had plenty of practice when it comes to loyalty. We are loyal to our family members, whether or not they have treated us well. We go to great lengths to show loyalty to our teams, clubs, and fraternities or sororities. We feel allegiance to our neighborhood, political party, religion, and country. This loyalty extents to all cultures; it allows us to "belong" and to be able to count on others.

We have different degrees and types of loyalty to each group to which we belong. The loyalty we have to a club is not the same as the loyalty we feel to our family. Yet, we can have allegiance to both. We may decide to completely ignore our self-interest to remain loyal to our family. Similarly, many have given their life for their country or religion. Whether we are aware of it or not, we are continually deciding how much loyalty to have toward one group or another.

As many of us have seen, one of the ongoing struggles that many families face is being torn between loyalty to family and to work. The workplace has certain expectations and so does the family; often they compete.

Many families come from cultures in which loyalty to family, cultural traditions, and religious practices is absolute throughout life. There is no question about which rules to follow. Modern parents watch as their children develop strong allegiances to their peer groups, and begin to follow the groups' rules. Unfortunately, the parents have known only one way, and that is absolute, unquestioned loyalty. The conflict between cultures can get pretty ugly if parents can't adjust to the new ways.

Loyalty can have rewards; it also can cause a great deal of grief and pain. For example, affiliation with a religious or cultural group has been known to be uplifting and give a positive sense of belonging; but it has also ended in the horrors of religious persecution and ethnic cleansing.

There is no "right" or "wrong" when it comes to rules about loyalty. Do we tell someone to no longer belong to a persecuted religion or political movement because this allegiance will cause him or her to be persecuted? Do we tell a soldier who is in a losing battle to go to the other side because his loyalty will be rewarded there? We accept that there is something about the many faces of loyalty that has made sense through the ages. There have been many payoffs. In fact, there is a mix of advantages and disadvantages regarding loyalty. We understand that having the loyalty of its members is necessary for any group to survive. Yet for new ideas to emerge, there need to be people who are willing and able to challenge the loyalty to an established order. The willingness of people to question and alter their degree of loyalty has led to the emergence of new ideas.

Often our loyalty experiences with family, religion, various peer groups, and our country impact our work life. We bring them to work with us and expect the same rules to apply. But whereas the rules of loyalty in the old workplace were more in line with traditional concepts of loyalty, the rules in the new workplace have changed dramatically.

Playing by the old loyalty rules when the workplace expects you to play by the new rules leads to one of the "Loyalty" traps. In this chapter, we offer practical solutions for breaking out of these traps. These solutions require skills and strategies that will be discussed in Part 2 of this book.

Traps from Too Much Loyalty

In the old work world, loyalty was key to success. It was the prize. Both employees and their organizations expected to give it and receive it. Today, however, expecting too much loyalty from your organization or from yourself can lead you into a personal trap. Here are some examples of how such traps can develop and what you can do to break free of them.

▶ **PERSONAL TRAP**

"They owe me"

Lauren was a hardworking buyer for a large department store chain where she had worked for fifteen years. Her work was typically high-pressured, and she took it seriously. There was neither trade show that she did not attend nor fashion trend that she was not on top of. Weekends were often spent just reading the latest fashion magazines. There was no season for a personal life.

Lauren enjoyed her job and appreciated all that her company had done for her—giving her the opportunity to do a job that she enjoyed and treating her well. She had learned a great deal at this job and believed she owed a lot to her company. Just as the company was counting on her, she knew she could count on it.

Lauren and her company grew closer. Her decisions directly affected garment sales. It was certain that her fate and her company's fate were one. Her social life was also entwined with the company. As a buyer, she had exposure to many people in many departments and locations. She was lucky that she had good friends in the company whom she could rely on and socialize with. It was really comforting to know that she was such an important part of this organization. It defined who she was.

Lauren was unable to foresee the disaster that was about to occur. Her company was taken over by an investor who bought up a majority of the stock. Suddenly the company was his. His first move was to find a way to pay off the tremendous debt he had incurred by buying this stock. This required many changes, including large-scale layoffs. Needless to say, Lauren's world turned upside down. There were lots of meetings, which resulted in a significant retrenchment of her department. Salaries were cut by 20 percent, and benefits were reduced. The previous atmosphere of cooperation and encouragement changed to one of demands and criticisms. To make matters worse, many of Lauren's co-workers and friends were laid off without even a thank-you for all their years of loyal service. The layoff survivors were seriously overworked and were clearly paying the price.

Lauren's disappointment and feelings of loss were overwhelming. Everything that was normal and familiar had changed overnight. This was not supposed to happen. Nothing made any sense. She had given her all to this company and had counted on it to take care of her. She kept thinking things would go back to "normal." If only she could get a decent night's sleep and get her appetite back. The constant tension and surges of sadness were also hard to deal with. How could she have given all of her loyalty to this company all these years? What about its loyalty to her? For now all she could do was fight to survive.

Remember Judith, the human resources manager from Chapter 1 with the "I Thought They Cared About Me" attitude? She had worked for her company for nineteen years and valued her personal relationship with the president. She had been told that she was one of the bright stars of the company. She had started with the company when it was small, and had worked endless hours as it had grown. She was sure the company could never have succeeded without her.

Judith took it for granted that she could always count on her president's loyalty to her, just he could always count on hers. As long as the president was there, she had a great booster and protector.

The company grew quickly and needed to create a vice president of human resources position. Judith had been promised that if the company ever grew large enough to need a vice president of human resources, the position would be hers. She really had what it took. She was valued.

But things changed. Competition became stiff and the company had to find a way to keep its market share and stay in business. A radical restructuring was implemented. There were more layoffs, departmental reorganizations, and other personnel changes. Unfortunately, one of those changes included the breaking of a promise: a vice president of human resources was hired from the outside. Judith was seen as too familiar and too aligned with the employees to implement the layoffs and the tough new personnel practices.

Judith was devastated. She could barely function at work. Her new boss was tough and piled the work on her without even asking for her input. She spent hours making sure that everything she did was perfect. She concentrated on protecting herself—after all, who else would hire her? Who would have the faith in her that the president had had? She had gotten where she was because she was special to him. He had given her a chance. Where was her protector now?

The trust Judith had had in the company was destroyed. Judith began to question herself, her abilities, and her judgment. If her loyal president had done this, there must be something wrong with her. How could he break his promise? Hadn't she been loyal?

▷ **STRATEGIC SOLUTION**

Cut your losses and move on

Despite the reality, Lauren and Judith were still looking for the company to be loyal to them. Lauren clung to the idea that it would all return to the old way. She spent her energy paying more dues than she needed to at work. Judith worked double time, operating under the assumption that she could do something to return to the old workplace, that her extraordinary effort would restore her old boss's loyalty toward her. Both Lauren and Judith were preoccupied with promises of the past and could see only hopelessness for the future.

It was time for Lauren and Judith to cut their losses and move on. They first needed to recognize that all was not lost. Their loyalty paid off in many ways. Lauren had learned the skills to become a successful buyer and had learned about the ins and outs of a major industry. She also had developed valuable organizational and people skills, as well as personal and professional contacts in a job that she enjoyed. She still had these skills.

Judith's loyalty had also brought her opportunities that she had seized. Her development and learning were impressive. She had started her job as a generalist and had learned all of the skills necessary to serve as a top-notch human resources professional. Her professional value increased and took her to a managerial level in a rapidly changing company. The work that she did was real; it had the value that merited the promise for the promotion. Her growth and ability to take on new challenges came from her unique ability, an ability that no one could take away.

The companies that Lauren and Judith were so loyal to no longer existed. This loss caused them very uncomfortable feelings associated with the grieving process. Lauren and Judith would find themselves in this grief process for a while and would need to take care of themselves. This includes doing things that would offer them comfort, seeking out the support of those who were close to them, and allowing themselves moments of sadness. If they could acknowledge the symbolic "death" of the old workplace, they could begin to participate in the new workplace in order to learn the new rules and try out new behaviors. The new loyalty rules focus on forwarding one's own self-interest and considering one's career goals while moving forward with the company.

▶ PERSONAL TRAP

"I'm going down with the ship"

Armando's years of working as a creative director in a midsize advertising agency had been very rewarding. The business was hectic, yet he could count on his boss, the president, to be fair and supportive. He was treated well and was learning from the job.

But Armondo could see the tide turning. There was significant business downturn in his area—once it started, it seemed to mushroom. Many of the small businesses that used outside advertising services either were being forced to close or had to cut their expenditures—including expenditures for advertising. Armando's company was losing business and having to drastically reduce its fees just to keep its accounts.

Armando offered to accept a salary cut in order to keep the cash flowing. He also worked extremely long hours just to help secure new business or service existing accounts. The pressure increased even more when some of his support staff were laid off. But Armando's only concern was for the company's survival. He had no thought of looking out for himself. As far as he was concerned, his well-being was the same as that of the company. He was absolutely loyal.

After all of this effort, he was shocked to learn from the president that the company was filing for bankruptcy and getting out with whatever revenue could be salvaged. It was difficult for Armando to stop his pace long enough to even hear this news, but once it sank in, he recognized that his loyalty had been betrayed. He realized that in order to file for bankruptcy, the president had to have been consulting with attorneys and accountants for a while. While he was doing this, he had encouraged Armando to lead the remaining loyal staff to sacrifice everything to save the company. Armando realized he had been duped. He felt like a fool. With all of this effort, he had not even imagined looking out for himself or his people.

▷ **STRATEGIC SOLUTION**

Separate your identity from the company's

Armando's loyalty was so absolute that he had totally identified the company's survival with his own. Remember Ana, the magazine proofreader with the "I've Put So Much into This Company" attitude whom you met in Chapter 1? When her company was sold, Ana decided to stay, against the advice of others, and "make it work." She had personally identified with the magazine's success, and refused to leave as a matter of pride. She was shocked and devastated when she was let go. Both Ana and Armando needed to recognize that when times were good they had been encouraged to develop strong loyalty bonds with their company and were rewarded for it. But the identification that they took on in the process had caused them to lose their own identity. Their feelings of responsibility took over. They had to save their world. Now, they needed to recognize that the outcome was ultimately not in their control, and their old world no longer existed.

Armando saw his company's failure as his own personal failure. Yet this long-held belief was being disproved before his very eyes: The company was dead, while he was still very much alive. Armando needed to separate his own image from that of the company. It was not his fault that the company had failed, that his employees were in this spot, that his customers were out on a limb. He needed to devote at least as much energy to his own survival as he had to his company's.

Armando worked on balancing his self-anger with self-praise. He reminded himself that he also had reason to applaud himself. He had to credit himself for the effort he had put forth. After all, it required a great deal of determination and skill. He could not control the market or the president's actions, but his actions had been heroic. He had managed to hold the operation together with his knowledge and experience. His employees had made the choice to hang in there just as he had. That was their decision even though they saw what was happening around them. He gave them the leadership they needed to keep going. He had much to be proud of.

Traps from Too Little Loyalty

Many people never recover from what they perceive to be a breach of loyalty. Once the company forsakes them, they make a decision, in one way or another, that they cannot risk being loyal to another company. They have to protect themselves from ever being hurt, betrayed, disappointed, or exploited again. In this section, we will meet some people who fell into traps by having too little loyalty and we will recommend some solutions.

▶ PERSONAL TRAP

"They burned me"

If a difficult assignment had to be done in the controller's office, Alex was there to do it. The company was important to him, and he worked hard to make the bottom line look good. He also knew that there was a solid career path for him. There were occasional openings for management positions in his department, and there were opportunities for advancement in other departments as well. All he had to do to get there was give his all.

But then Alex's company merged with a smaller company. Clearly there were not going to be two controller's offices. Suddenly all of the rules changed. Everybody was tense as the big decisions were being made. Alex did not give up—after all, these changes required the leadership of people who knew what they were doing. He had worked hard to prove that he was one of them.

The new company decided to keep Alex's manager in the position of controller. As a compromise to the smaller company, the next two management positions were given to its people; Alex would stay on as a staff member. The chance for the dreamed promotion that he had worked for was now very remote.

Alex could barely stomach the fact that what he had sacrificed and worked so hard for was now no longer possible. There was no other employee as loyal as he was. He was angry with everyone, but especially with the controller for whom he had "slaved" all these years. Alex believed his manager could have fought to have him promoted, even if it required creating a new position. The longer he thought about it, the angrier he became. He tried to do his work but found it increasingly difficult to concentrate. He wondered how he could do anything more for this company that had betrayed him after all that he had done for it.

Alex could not let go of his rage. Why had he given this company his all? Didn't he know any better? He could have pursued other opportunities. Now it was too late. He was lost and had feelings that he had never had before. He began to have headaches, stomach problems, and sleepless nights. He could not enjoy his family or friends. He was preoccupied with his pain—both emotional and physical.

The only way he could see to get some peace was to get something back. He would take his time doing assignments. No matter how crunched they were, he would no longer be available to stay late or take work home. He also withheld any suggestions that might be helpful for the new managers. He felt pleasure every time he noticed that they were making mistakes, particularly if it embarrassed them or his old boss. He took any opportunity to demean the new management by pointing out their mistakes and unfairness to co-workers. His anger and bitterness drove his actions. Unfortunately, this bitterness was spilling into the rest of his life as well.

▷ STRATEGIC SOLUTION

Think "payoff" not "payback"

Alex needed to recognize that he was holding himself hostage as a payback for his loyalty. He had been loyal with the express purpose of getting ahead in the company. His loyalty had always had a return clause in it as far as he was concerned. His measure was what he would get back. Now that the plan was thwarted, he could not tolerate the fact that he wasn't where he had expected to be. He wasn't getting the payback.

In all of his getting even, Alex gave up on his career goals and ambitions. All of his energy was spent being stuck and negative. He was actually getting used to this as a normal way of thinking and doing things. Alex needed to recognize that actions taken out of bitterness will only backfire. Getting even might give him immediate relief; however, it might also sabotage his career. Remember Daniel, the computer salesman you met in Chapter 1 with the "Why Should I Bother?" attitude? When his company began to lose money, they cut his commission. His anger and personal disappointment became greater with time, and he became less motivated to please his customers. He did not wake up to the reality of what he was doing until one of his best accounts threatened to withdraw. Like Daniel, Alex was becoming the architect of his own destruction. The more he tried to get even with the bad guys, the more damage he would do to himself. He would be judged a poor team player with little to offer or, at best, as a poor to mediocre player who had little value. The only payoff for these behaviors would be to lose whatever advantage he might have had from having allies serve his self-interest. He was ruining any chance for a payoff in the future.

Alex needed to turn his loyalty to himself and his own future. He needed to appreciate what his loyalty had achieved for him and use it for his future. Up until the change (which neither he nor his old manager could control), he had had the respect and loyalty of his manager and colleagues. He also had added a great deal of value to himself as a professional. Why not cash in on these gains? Why not focus on continuing to add value?

This strategy requires that Alex target his loyalty toward his current bosses with a purpose. This time he must do it with the goal of self-interest. His focus should be on advancing his career, and he must not remain hostage to this one company. He needs to enlist his new managers in his effort to advance his career goals. As he does this, he will seize any opportunities for growth and perhaps internal opportunities. He can also begin a campaign that extends beyond his company. This includes seeking out as much professional exposure as possible, relevant retraining, and career development. In the second part of this book, we will discuss how to acquire some of these skills.

▶ PERSONAL TRAP

"I'm waiting for the other shoe to drop"

Let's revisit Charles, the hardworking plant manager in Chapter 1 with the "I Won't Let This Happen Again" attitude. When the company took an unexpected downturn, the pressure was on. Charles's boss became very tough and demanding. Suddenly Charles, who had prided himself on his excellence, could do nothing right.

Charles began looking for signs of another disaster. He was haunted by the fear that suddenly the other shoe would drop. He couldn't tolerate it. Whenever he heard a negative rumor it caused him to pull back and overtook him with fear. He no longer could identify with the company. He was reluctant to put in the amount of time and effort that he had in the past, and even openly questioned whether such involvement was worth his while. How could he stand another betrayal? He felt he had to hold back.

▷ **STRATEGIC SOLUTION**

Cultivate loyalty with a purpose

Charles was protecting himself from the possibility of further painful betrayal. This attitude trapped him into focusing on how to completely avoid this awful fate in the future. He began to believe that loyalty was so risky that it had to be avoided. He began to do things that were against his self-interest. His unwillingness to put in the extra effort on behalf of the company and his open skepticism would certainly not impress his employees, his managers, or his colleagues. He was no longer likely to gain the respect that he was capable of garnering and had garnered in the past.

Charles learned something about loyalty that he would always remember: Loyalty is not absolute; it can be taken away at any moment. Loyalty cannot be assumed to last forever. That does not mean that it did not pay off; rather, he had to learn how to use loyalty with a purpose, to forward his own self-interest.

Charles's self-interest would be served by gaining the respect of his management and co-workers. They were looking to him for loyalty to their common efforts and to join them in achieving success. If he hoped to have whatever payoffs and rewards were there, he would need to demonstrate some degree of loyalty. Only this time, he would know why he was giving it.

Charles needed to learn to choose the loyalty level that was best for him. Loyalty is not an all-or-nothing thing. The fact that it changed and there was a loss does not take away the value of aligning with the company and its mission. Charles could have loyalty to himself and his company at the same time. His job now is to use his loyalty skills to get a payoff in his current position. He will only get that payoff if he does the things that make his manager, employees, and co-workers see that *their* self-interest is served by maintaining loyalty to him. This will not happen if he is stingy with his time and availability, skeptical, and negative.

He needs to be supportive, appreciative, and as helpful as possible. If his boss sees that Charles can serve his self-interest, he may develop loyalty to Charles in turn. This may provide opportunities for Charles to grow in the company, expand his contacts, gain knowledge of career opportunities in other companies, develop skills, and perhaps even pursue formal training. On the other hand, if the boss is unable to return his loyalty, Charles can use this time to seek out other opportunities without having all of his energy stuck in a direction that will not pay off.

Charles knows how to be effectively loyal because he has already done it. But this time he has to hold some reserve that will keep him safe in case of reversals. He must put some limits on himself to prevent being fully enveloped by his company. Having other professional involvement and affiliations and a balanced life outside of his company is important. The company can capture his skill, but not him. His loyalty to any company is dependent upon its need for him and his need for the company. If the rules change, he will be ready.

Absolute Versus Relative Loyalty

Our friends were confused about the loyalty rules in their company. When times were good, they were encouraged to develop a very personal loyalty bond with the company. Their loyalty was rewarded. They were loyal to the company, and the company took care of their self-interest. The problem arose when the company that they were loyal to went through a drastic change. At that point the loyalty rules also changed. Their value to the company was determined by how they fit into the company's new plan. Now they needed to figure out what was *their* new plan.

We believe that there is a middle ground when it comes to loyalty. You can learn how to have your loyalty work for you during the good times and the bad. You can make choices about your loyalty and can actually use loyalty to your advantage. You can have loyalty with a purpose—loyalty that forwards the company's self-interest.

Loyalty is the glue that keeps people connected with their company and helps them get whatever benefits they can. Employees' knowledge that their company would always be equally loyal to them fueled the absolute loyalty of the old workplace. The new workplace has brought a degree of unpredictability. You may get a return on your loyalty investment, but it is not the same as in the past. The loyalty of an employee will be reciprocated—to a degree—by the company, its management, and the person's colleagues; but loyalty is relative to the current situation and has little to do with the allegiances of yesterday. The concept of loyalty in the new workplace is not based on rules of reciprocity.

In order to apply the new loyalty rules, you need to be able to direct your loyalty in several directions at once. You can no longer afford to direct all of your allegiance to your company. There is no need to feel guilt for not giving your company all of your loyalty; chances are it does not want it anyway. Successful people do what they have to do. They adjust to the change.

The following exercise will help you determine whether you are an "absolute loyalist" or you have the relative loyalty skills that are needed to break out of the "Loyalty" trap.

TRAP BREAKER

Loyalty

Are you an absolute loyalist? Answer the following questions "True" or "False" and find out.

Absolute Loyalist

	True	False
If I give my allegiance and skills, I can count on the company to support and reward me.	___	___
If the company promises rewards for my loyalty and hard work, I am guaranteed a bright future with the company.	___	___
If I do a good job, my future with the company is secure.	___	___
If this is a good company to work for, I can count on that continuing.	___	___

If you answered "True" to any of the previous statements, you may be trapped by expectations of absolute loyalty. We call it a trap because times have changed, especially in relation to loyalty. It's no longer absolute; it's relative. This means that you need to add some new skills to your repertoire. We call these the relative loyalty skills. These are the skills for today's workplace. Where do you stand as a relative loyalist?

Relative Loyalist

	True	False
I can recognize the difference between company loyalty and career loyalty.	____	____
I feel it is important to mix loyalty to the company with loyalty to myself.	____	____
I have multiple loyalties at the same time.	____	____
I can withdraw loyalty from my company, if necessary, without jeopardizing the company bond.	____	____
I can recognize when my loyalty investment will not be returned.	____	____
I can develop allegiance with one company while maintaining the ability to shift loyalties when necessary.	____	____
I put a higher priority on being loyal to my career than to my company.	____	____
When there are reversals or downturns in the company, I remain flexible and am willing to shift gears without resentment.	____	____
I know that it is necessary to persuade the company to be loyal to me, and I know how I can do so.	____	____

The more "True" answers you were able to give to the above questions, the better are your loyalty skills connected to success in any company or work situation. You can use these skills, or work on developing them, to help you succeed in the new workplace.

Chapter 6

The "We're Just One Big Family" Traps

It is not uncommon to hear employees describe their workplace relationships in family terms: "We're just like family"; "They're more of a family to me than my own family"; or "I spend more time with them than with my at-home family."

In her book *Home Away from Home,* Janet Woititz talks about the workplace as resembling a family unit. She compares the relationship between the one who gives orders (manager) and the one who takes orders (employee) to that between parent and child and the relationship between co-workers to that between siblings (see Figure 1).

Woititz would say that our relational patterns at work are very similar to those we have experienced in our family. If we had a very difficult time with a parent, we may experience some of the same difficulty with a manager. If we had a conflict or competitive relationship with a sibling, we may duplicate it with a co-worker. Our experiences in the role of parent may carry over into the workplace, causing us in the role of manager to feel, for example, either overly responsible for or mistrustful toward our employees.

FIGURE 1

WORKPLACE AS FAMILY

Workplace		Family
Workplace		*Family*
Manager	⸺⸺⸺➤	Parent
Co-workers	⸺⸺⸺➤	Siblings
Employee	⸺⸺⸺➤	Child

Here are some quotes from people who have carried over their family relational patterns into the workplace:

Parental approval seeker: I used to like being with my manager because he gave me positive feedback. Now, with the new pressures, I can't seem to please him. It's very unfair. I'm beginning to believe that he doesn't like me. Now I find myself spending too much time being upset with him.

Sibling in rivalry: Look at how he cozies up to management. He gets away with murder. I do the work, and he gets the recognition. I can't stand it. It's unfair. Why is he getting all of the recognition? What about me?

Parent having trouble letting go: I just can't trust them. They don't have the experience that I do. I feel like I have to watch over them every minute or they may make a big mistake, and I'll be responsible for it. If they lose their jobs, it will be my fault.

Often people have the same expectations of their work relationships that they have of their relationships at home. They may be reliving some of the same struggles they had with their family. These family dynamics are not typically in a person's self-interest and can get in the way of effectiveness at work. There should be no mistaking the relationships—a manager is a manager, not a parent; a co-worker is just that, not a sister or brother; the people one manages are employees, not children.

Employee relationships have become even more strained as a result of the changes in the workplace of today. This results in a heightened energy that can be very powerful and consuming. With all of this on-the-job contact, working relationships seem to become very personal. Thus it is important to be aware of traps that you can fall into because of your job role. In this chapter, we will show you how to avoid or get out of these traps, and we will help you relate to your workplace players appropriately.

Relationship Traps with Your Manager

Managers have power. They also have responsibilities for which they must be accountable. They are messengers for upper management, who expects them to pass down the work to frontline workers. If the job is done well, the goal is achieved and the manager is credited; if not, the manager is blamed.

In exchange for this responsibility, upper management gives the manager a great deal of power over our work lives. Your manager is responsible for assigning the projects and evaluating performance. Most important, he or she is also the one who can help you shine your light or put a damper on it. Part of being effective as an employee is succeeding with this important person. As far as you are concerned, he or she *is* the company. Your manager relies on you as well—to get the job done and to enable him or her to be successful as a leader. You can use this fact to your advantage.

Employees in today's changing workplace often have to deal with managers who are delivering a much more demanding message than in previous times. This often causes them to get stuck in certain traps. We will look at some of the more common ones.

▶ **PERSONAL TRAP**

"I am at my manager's mercy"

Reiko spent years as production manager of a small record company, and she had been a major player in its success. The company became so successful that it was an attractive prospect for a purchase. The acquiring company was much more impersonal and results oriented than the original company. Someone who was much sterner and more demanding replaced Reiko's boss—her decisions were constantly being challenged; prices from suppliers were never low enough; she was always moving slower than she should; an agreed-upon deadline would be shortened unexpectedly. When an idea that Reiko had presented and her manager had put down resurfaced as the manager's own, Reiko felt she had had enough. It was clear that this new player had no stake in Reiko's continued success. She spent most of her time dealing with feelings that ranged from rage to frustration to bewilderment to fear and panic. Reiko was able to admit that her personal reactions were magnified by the ghost of an authority figure from the past who had no place in her current reality.

Reed worked for a midsize manufacturing company. He reported to a manager who often got lost in details and would become very angry when certain mistakes were made. At other times Reed was told how valuable he was. When the pressure was on, Reed was on the receiving end of some brutal criticism. His morale was sinking fast and he felt that he had to do something.

He chose a moment when things were going well between him and his manager. He used a very direct approach. He started by letting his manager know how much he appreciated their positive interactions. He then explained the impact that some of the angry sessions had had on him. Reed made it clear that he valued their working relationship and that his comments were meant to improve it. Reed's manager was not aware of the negative impact his behavior had on Reed. Reed was surprised when the manager resolved to change. This resulted in a real improvement in their working relationship.

Within a year things changed in the company. The manager was clearly in a pressure cooker as his department was not meeting the increasingly demanding production schedules. Once again he became very abusive and insensitive to Reed's reactions. When Reed approached him again, he received a very different reception. Reed was reminded about the pressures. He was accused of not being a team player, being petty when the chips were down, and being plain disloyal. The manager wondered if he could count on him during these tough times. Reed left feeling very disheartened. He also began to notice that he was being assigned less important tasks and his compliant co-workers were getting many of the assignments that Reed would have gotten in the past. He questioned the wisdom of his direct approach strategy.

▷ **STRATEGIC SOLUTION**

Take responsibility for yourself

Reiko needed to see her personal reactions as intruders that she had to deal with to succeed. She had to get clear about the idea that her manager was not the authority figure from her past and let go of the personal aspects of the relationship. Only then would she be confident enough to develop a strategy.

It was clear that Reiko's manager had the power. She decided that her success depended on enlisting him to be on her team. To succeed in this situation, she would have to take action that would give her manager what he needed. By doing this, she would further her own position. Reiko had to begin to see her manager as someone whom *she was now managing.*

Reiko decided to appeal to her manager's self-interest. She tried to get a sense of what he needed and then worked on figuring out how to give it to him. She concluded that her manager needed to feel that he was in control and that he had all the ideas. She was careful not to challenge or threaten him. Eventually Reiko was able to make her manager see her as someone whom he wanted in that position.

We are not suggesting that Reiko resign herself to this position forever. This is a temporary strategy. As situations change and it is in her self-interest, she will need to modify or change her strategy. But for now, she has decided to work on increasing her workplace value while being alert to other opportunities both within and outside the company. She has taken responsibility for herself.

Reed needed to remember not to take his manager's mood swings personally. He had to get off that roller coaster and decide what was important to him. He had to take responsibility for himself.

Reed established some clear goals for himself and worked on finding ways to achieve them. In the meantime, he reevaluated the direct approach, which had positive results the first time, but not the second.

Here are some guidelines for using the direct approach with your manager:

☑ Be friendly, not confrontational, avoiding inflammatory words or other references that might result in defensiveness.

☑ Focus on the positive; use examples of what is working.

☑ Share information with the manager about his or her behaviors that make it harder for you to work effectively, but be sure to give the benefit of the doubt by acknowledging that the manager probably didn't realize this was happening.

☑ Ask for feedback about things that you do that concern him or her. Be prepared to hear that your manager's behavior might be a reaction to your behaviors.

☑ Be ready for a cooperative agreement.

☑ Be prepared for the possibility that your manager may start a shoot-out. If so, you know who will win. Retreat and minimize the damage.

As you can see, the direct approach is worth trying, but it also carries some risk. Before you consider it, observe your manager's approach and interactions to see how he or she is likely to respond

▶ **PERSONAL TRAP**

"I can't let my manager down"

Zach was an administrative assistant in a chemical company. His manager, who was responsible for new product development, was juggling more assignments than usual. She was trying to gear up in response to rumors that a competitor was working on a product that would be a threat to the company's operation. Given the gravity of the situation, she had to assign some of the important investigations to her assistants. She turned to Zach to do some market research. She gave him a short deadline and let him know that she was counting on him.

Zach was overwhelmed by the amount of material he had to look over. Yet, he was determined to come through for his manager and prove himself. In order to meet the deadline, he cut corners and was not as thorough as he normally would have been. As time passed and the deadline approached, Zach moved more quickly and cut more corners. He was not sure whether some of the guessing he was doing was acceptable, but he did not want his manager to lose faith in him. He had to do it; he couldn't let her down.

Zach got the report to his manager by the deadline. She was grateful and proceeded to review what Zach had done. The next day, the report came back to him covered with red ink. Much of the information he had provided was incomplete or incorrect. The manager had to turn to another administrative assistant to clean it up.

▷ STRATEGIC SOLUTION

Take responsibility for your work

Zach learned a very valuable lesson. A manager who gives him flexibility is taking a risk on him. However, any manager should be able to count on employees to do what they say they will do. Managers justifiably expect high-caliber work regardless of time problems. Zach learned that he needed to keep his manager informed and to take responsibility for what he produced. It was his responsibility to tell his manager if he needed help or more guidance to finish the assignment. No manager can afford to be surprised at the last minute. The work that you do becomes your responsibility and reflects on your credibility.

Relationship Traps with Your Co-Workers

When the workplace undergoes change, what once seemed like a harmonious place can become a war zone plagued with relationship traps. New rules of competition may leave people feeling personally attacked. Employees get trapped into isolation, distrust, and pettiness at the very time when they need to learn to shift gears and develop different types of relationships with one another. Let's look at what can happen.

▶ **PERSONAL TRAP**

"I keep hearing rumors"

Rosette was a chemist working for a chemical manufacturing company. She liked worked for the company. The business was stable, the owners were fair and considerate of employees' needs, the environment was friendly and supportive, and she considered her co-workers to be among her best friends. Rosette worked hard and felt justly rewarded financially. She was glad to be part of a company that was profitable and in which her efforts meant something.

During her eighth year with the company, Rosette began hearing rumors that the owner was planning to retire. Although he didn't validate the information, the rumor persisted. It seemed that he was looking tired and taking more time off. Maybe he *was* going to retire. What would happen to the company? A new rumor spread that the owner would sell to a larger company and take the financial rewards. Where would that leave the employees? Rosette spent her lunch and breaks discussing the rumors. Between the rumors and the talk in the office, she was so distressed that it affected her ability to function. She couldn't imagine herself working anywhere else, but should she start looking for a new job? Now, unfortunately, if there were a change, her deteriorating job performance wouldn't stand her in good stead.

Don had worked on the support staff of a food distributor for several years. He wasn't crazy about the job, but it offered him fair compensation and he had positive relationships with his co-workers. Then a rumor began to spread that most of the support work was going to be done in the company's central location, hundreds of miles away. Each day a new rumor cropped up citing one more reason for this and one more action that was being taken to make it happen. Don couldn't escape the rumor mill and became panicky about the implications for him. He couldn't move his family to the other side of the country, nor could he survive without a job. What if he had to go looking for another job while competing with his co-workers? After all, there weren't that many jobs around. He quickly made calls out to the few distributorships in the area and took the first offer that came to him. It was with a less desirable firm with fewer opportunities and a slight reduction in pay. However, at least he was safe.

▷ STRATEGIC SOLUTION

Maintain your perspective

We often talk with people who are surrounded by rumors at work. The information they receive in this way is often frightening and tends to build on itself. Despite the fact that the information is anonymous, unsubstantiated, and unreliable, those who hear it often take hasty, impulsive action that is not in their best interest.

The information Rosette was getting threatened a work world that was very important to her. Her worries about this impending great loss and what it would mean for her crippled her ability to function. Don was consumed by the rumors circulating in his workplace and his thoughts about the disaster that was going to follow. He couldn't tolerate the idea that he might be without work. He felt he had no choice but to find security elsewhere, even at a loss to himself.

Both Rosette and Don were victims of the rumor mill. Because they were so focused on it, they couldn't help being affected by it. They needed to treat this rumor mill as just what it was—an unsubstantiated information source. It is probably safe to assume that some of what they were hearing was true. But the information was emotionally loaded and therefore had a greater than normal chance of being exaggerated.

How do you take care of yourself while in the midst of this process? Certainly you would want to stay connected with your co-workers and not pull away. You could become the group detective. What would you want to find out? You could begin with the following questions: Who is the source of the information? What exactly did he or she say? What is his or her level of certainty? How sure is he or she of the information? What is his or her basis? Are there other possible explanations? Are there other sources of information who have a different point of view?

Let's say that these rumors have some validity. Remember that you have control over whether they will cause you emotional distress or whether you will invoke reason and logic. You may logically decide to use this as the impetus to launch a carefully crafted job search. Don't forget to utilize some of the skills in Chapters 8 and 12.

▶ **PERSONAL TRAP**

"If not for him I would be fine"

The word was out. Changes were coming. The company was looking at ways to run more efficiently and all departments were being examined. Some growth was also anticipated, which meant there might be some additional job opportunities. Jeremy, who always hoped for advancement, saw this as an opportunity to show his stuff. However, he began to notice that several of his co-workers were regularly beating him to the punch. They seemed to be spending extra time with his manager and getting special recognition for work they were doing. In fact, often when a new assignment emerged, Jeremy's partner was the first to jump up and seize it.

Jeremy was a strong team player and liked to work with people. He just couldn't be cutthroat or intentionally "one-up" someone else. Increasingly upset by the competitiveness where there had been collaboration, Jeremy felt himself giving up. He even began to doubt his ability as he watched the spotlight continue to shine on his co-workers. After a while he found it difficult to concentrate and accomplish his assignments.

▷ **STRATEGIC SOLUTION**

Be clear about your place

Jeremy was caught in a position in which the rules had quickly changed and he couldn't adapt to them. He had a cooperative style and was an excellent team player, and he had flourished in the company until now. But in the new dog-eat-dog environment, he was not able to function. He just wasn't that aggressive. For him, the type of battling required to succeed was uncomfortable to say the least.

Jeremy needed to change his understanding of his place at work. The environment had become competitive. There would be winners and losers. And the game was being decided within a short time frame. Jeremy needed to decide whether to stay and play by the new rules or develop an exit strategy. If he decided to stay, he would need to learn the rules and skills of competition.

One of the rules, as we've mentioned, is that there are winners and losers. Jeremy could be one or the other. If he chose to win he would need to decide where his strengths lay and do whatever he could to make them shine, either by taking on special projects or by somehow showcasing his unique contribution. It wouldn't hurt for him to meet with his supervisor alone and discuss his performance and the contributions he could make. If his competitors tried to intrude, he would need to assertively establish his place as discussed in *Your Perfect Right* (Alberti and Emmons, 1995). He would need to put in all the time he could to achieve, and seek out assistance if he needed it to excel. He also needed to keep his eyes open to new opportunities and quickly make it clear that he could and would take them on. If he felt bad about this process, he needed to remind himself that he was competing just as his co-workers were.

Relationship Traps When You Are the Manager

▶ PERSONAL TRAP

"I take care of my people"

Eve supervised a team of auditors in an insurance company. One of her team members began to come to work late on a daily basis. When she approached him he mentioned that he had household responsibilities and problems. She was sympathetic to his problems, but told him he had to be at work on time. After her warning, the employee managed to appear on time for several days, but then he reverted back to his old behavior. Eve noticed that he spent time daydreaming at his desk, but she didn't want it to seem like she was adding to his problems. She was very empathetic. Moreover, she remembered that he had always been very supportive of her when the going was tough. The employee was also respected and liked by his co-workers, and Eve felt his presence was important to team morale.

It wasn't long before the employee started making critical mistakes in his work. Eve felt a need to check all of his work before it went on to the next step. She had discussions with him that she hoped would help him improve. Immediately after these discussions, he would improve and do superior work. But a few weeks would go by, and he would revert back to his old ways. Eve began to feel like she was on an emotional roller coaster, depending on how her employee was doing. She wanted to keep him and was willing to invest the time and energy needed to work with him, but her method of dealing with the situation was clearly taking a toll on her. When it came to evaluations, she always tried to stress the positives in his performance. She wanted to motivate him, not discourage him. She kept convincing herself that she was doing this for the sake of the team. She could hardly allow herself to acknowledge that her main concern was personal. She had begun to take personal responsibility for his survival on the job.

Then the house of cards fell down. As the demands for productivity increased, it became clear that all employees had to pull their own weight. The pressure was on. Other departments were showing the strain and sharing their concerns with Eve. She became angry when she saw the price she and her team were paying to make up for one employee's lack of productivity.

Eve recognized that she would have to change and apply the rules. As she became more demanding of her employee to do his job, he became hostile and indignant. He reminded her that he hadn't changed his performance, and that he had always received a satisfactory rating. Why the change now? He decided that this was unfair and that he would not let this drop. After all, he had his rights. Eve also noticed that he was having long, whispered conversations with his team members and that she was getting a colder reception from them. It was clear that his team members would protect one of their own, and that didn't include her.

Eve had gotten herself into a very embarrassing situation. After all, she had allowed him to do an unsatisfactory job and had never held him responsible for his performance. Now her only recourse was to take managerial action and use the power of the position.

She had to hope that her management wouldn't judge her too harshly for having let her employee slack off. After undergoing some humiliating questioning, she was referred to human resources for guidance. It was clear that she had a real problem with changing the rules. She could not do much to discipline her employee without having a record of a pattern of poor performance. His record, written by her, reflected satisfactory performance. Now he was going to use this against her. It was clear that Eve had been acting more like a parent than a manager and, as a result, had inadequately supervised an unsatisfactory employee.

Remember Reiko? Her manager had a different role problem. He criticized her every decision and had her redo her work. After rejecting Reiko's ideas, he would later present them as his own. He needed to be lord and master. This tendency increased as the pressure and uncertainty increased. He constantly had to show that he had superior knowledge, full power, and full control. He could never let anyone see any of his vulnerabilities, uncertainties, or problems. He spent endless hours micromanaging Reiko. For him, the only way to win was to be on top of everything.

Reiko was very creative and hardworking, but she began to feel that she might as well just sit around and watch her manager do her work. She certainly wasn't inspired to do her best since she believed it would be rejected anyway.

Meanwhile, the manager was headed for certain burnout. If he continued to put pressure on himself to constantly prove that he was superior and in command, he would have to closely supervise every product that was produced by his team. Instead of getting the fruits of his team's best efforts, he was limiting their productivity by reviewing everything and worrying about something getting past him.

▷ **STRATEGIC SOLUTION**

Be clear about your role

Eve learned a valuable lesson the hard way. Her role was not to "take care of her people." Her role was to be upper management's messenger and, as such, to ensure that her employees got the job done.

Eve needed to clearly present her expectations to her employees and work on motivating and coaching her team to meet them. Having regular meetings to discuss individual and team progress and identify potential problems was essential. If a performance problem were identified, she needed to analyze the nature of the problem and offer any necessary special training, support, and opportunities for improvement. Follow-up to monitor progress was also critical. If the person were still not performing satisfactorily, it would be necessary for her to do one of the hardest things for most managers to do: document performance problems in writing and develop a formal plan for improvement. It would be essential for ongoing reviews and evaluations to accurately reflect the person's progress or lack thereof.

Eve came to realize that there are consequences for not keeping an eye on job performance. She spent her workdays worrying about the personal problems of her employee and covering for his poor performance. As a result, she unwittingly communicated the message that it's all right to let personal problems interfere with job performance. When the pressure was on and she tried to change the rules, her nurturing relationship changed suddenly into an adversarial one. The employee she stopped "protecting" used all of the ammunition he could to protect himself.

Remember Benesha, whom you met in Chapter 1? She was the manager with the "I No Longer Have Any Friends" attitude who had trouble accepting her role as a manager. She learned her lesson very quickly—the hard way. As you may recall, during a difficult time she was promoted to supervise the team of which she had been a member. She was now delivering management's difficult messages of change. As she delivered these messages, it became clear that her former co-workers saw her as the enemy and identified with and supported one another—not her. The team members saw that what could happen to one of them could happen to any of them. Benesha was seen as management's enforcer. She also became the focus of her team's frustration and anger. Suddenly she was shut out and alone. Benesha's solution was to join with the other managers, all of whom were in the same spot. Sharing similar experiences, pressures, suggestions, and solutions with others in similar situations helped her clarify her new role as a manager and begin acting like one.

As a manager, your role is different from that of your team members. It is in your self-interest to remember this. We have known managers who, in their frustration, shared their anger about the company openly with their employees. Unfortunately, these managers found that the employees used this openness against them at a later time. We have also seen many instances in which managers inappropriately shared with their employees their disagreement with a particular policy. Too often, this resulted in resentment, distrust, and disrespect for the manager when he or she then attempted to enforce the policy. The employees had the attitude that they need not heed the policy if their own manager didn't believe in it.

Reiko's "lord and master" will need to learn how to win by being the leader of a winning team—by managing his people, not controlling them. He needs to do the following:

- ☑ Manage his people
- ☑ Let them do their jobs
- ☑ Motivate his people to do their best
- ☑ Offer support and training as needed
- ☑ Make sure his people get the job done
- ☑ Measure his effectiveness by how productive his people are
- ☑ Recognize that his team can achieve more than he can
- ☑ Recognize that he is successful if each of his people is successful
- ☑ Remember that being successful is supporting his team members' becoming successful
- ☑ Remember that he is not successful if his team members are not doing their jobs as effectively as they could
- ☑ Recognize that his success depends on the team's success

If you are not clear about your role, your team certainly will not be clear. If you do not present the standard, how will the team know it? If you are preoccupied with an employee's personal problems, how can you manage your team and be your company's messenger? If you have to control everything, how can you have the focus to manage your team? To be successful in the role of manager, you must be clear about what that role is.

▶ **PERSONAL TRAP**

"It's all my fault"

Like overprotective parents, managers who tend to be too person-ally invested in their employees' lives often suffer from guilt. In these times of change, layoffs and career disappointments are not uncommon. Even when managers are not a part of the decision making regarding who will be laid off, as messengers of upper management, they have to deliver the bad news to their team members. Often they respond like a guilty parent—they feel their employees' problems are their fault.

We have seen the same guilt in incidents in which an accident or other workplace tragedy resulted in employee injury or death. Of course, this guilt is compounded when there are also layoffs and increased workloads. While the causes of tragedy in the workplace vary, the manager's reactions are often the same. If an overburdened employee suffers a heart attack, the manager is often convinced that it's because he or she pushed the employee too hard. If there is an accident, the manager feels certain that there must have been a way to have taken care of that safety concern, altered the assignment, or done something—anything—to have prevented the accident.

Matt was a district sales manager for a computer equipment company. He had a reputation for working hard and for motivat-ing his sales people to meet his expectations. He also cared about his employees. One day, one of his sales representatives had a fatal car accident while in the field. Matt became seriously depressed. Although he had been in his office twenty miles away when the accident happened and could not have done anything to prevent it, Matt felt tremendously guilty. He could not get past the feeling that he was somehow personally responsible and, had he done something differently, his employee would be alive today.

▷ STRATEGIC SOLUTION

Be clear about your responsibility

Matt felt responsible for everything that happened to his team members. As a manager, he already had plenty of pressure and responsibility. He became overburdened and depressed when he took on responsibility for things that were beyond his control. Matt needed to be clear about where his responsibility as a manager began and ended. Matt and other guilt-ridden managers would do well to remember this. A manager's responsibility is limited and includes the following:

☑ Delivering upper management's messages to employees   ✓
☑ Making sure employees have the training and tools to do their ✓ job
☑ Making sure employees perform their job as expected   ✓
☑ Making sure that the working environment adheres to specified safety standards   ✓
☑ Delivering the employees' messages back to upper management   ✓

A manager is *not* responsible for the following:

☑ Preventing employees from failing, slacking off, or making mistakes
☑ Solving employees' personal problems
☑ Preventing unexpected accidents that occur within an environment in which safety standards are maintained
☑ Ensuring that employees do not have negative reactions to their work assignments
☑ Taking responsibility for the personal consequences of an employee's layoff

▶ **PERSONAL TRAP**

"I'm stuck in the middle"

Jake had been a top team player throughout his career. When the company began to expand, it needed more management people. This was Jake's opportunity to advance and become manager of a unit. The problem was that, once he was promoted, he was given very little guidance as to how to do his job. Jake's manager was spread thin and barely had any time for him. The only thing he told Jake was that his team had a quota to achieve—"Just do it!" If Jake had to do some of the work himself, so be it. It was clear that if the quota wasn't met, he was the one who would be blamed. If he asked how to push his team to meet the quota goals, he was told to figure it out. He knew that if his team members didn't produce he should "write them up." To make matters worse, Jake was told that other teams were achieving over their projected goals. In addition to all his other work, it seemed like Jake had an endless stream of reports to complete for his manager. He found that he had to take reports home and do them during the evening or on weekends. This was the only way he knew to keep his head above water.

Not only did Jake have to deal with this lack of direction, he also had to deal with his team's reactions. His employees saw him as the bad guy who was imposing an impossible burden on them. Moreover, they often had different ideas about how the job should be done and did not seem to respect Jake's opinions. Jake's confusion about his manager's messages carried over into his messages to his employees.

Jake felt trapped in the middle. He was angry and ready to quit.

▷ STRATEGIC SOLUTION

Be clear about your message

As a manager you are truly in the middle. You find out what upper management's message is and then deliver it to your employees. This means that you report to a boss and have all of the challenges that any employee has. On the other hand, you have to lead a team of subordinates. At times you might also have to produce your own work product as well.

Before you can carry upper management's message to your troops, you have to be ready to own it as yours. Otherwise, you can't expect your team to take it seriously. You must be clear about the message. To do this, you need to interact and communicate effectively with your own manager. After all, he or she is the one who will evaluate your work and take responsibility for your results.

A good working relationship and good communication with your manager are important. Here are some points we think will help you. These points are all based on the assumption that not only is your manager responsible for your team's results, but because he or she is often dealing with critical areas, problems, and "putting out fires," your manager will not have too much time to focus on you.

So when you interact with your manager, make it count. Here are some points to remember before a meeting:

☑ Think about what you need from your manager and about what your manager can give you.

☑ Gear your meeting toward solutions.

☑ Ask for clarification of goals, guidelines, and priorities that will help you complete your project.

☑ Identify special problems that may affect your manager as the one who is responsible for work activities. Present your concerns or possible problems with clear action implications.

☑ Let your manager know about the type of support you need from him or her. Do this early on in the project to give your manager needed time, especially if it involves staffing, equipment, or safety.

☑ Leave your disagreements at the door. Don't forget you are your manager's messenger and it is his or her message you are being paid to disseminate.

☑ Share words of understanding, thanks, and encouragement. Don't forget that your manager is also a messenger with a difficult middle position.

Finding Your Place in the Puzzle

As you have seen, the workplace is no longer one big happy family (not that it ever really was) with a patriarch or matriarch and rarely a divorce. It is now more a marriage of partners with a prenuptial agreement that says that each partner brings something and each partner receives something. If that arrangement changes, or if for other reasons the relationship no longer meets the one or the other's needs, or if outside forces result in the arrangement not being in either partner's self-interest, the relationship can be terminated.

In the workplace, the labor is divided among various players, each with a different set of skills and a special position or role. The manager is upper management's messenger or representative; the people who carry out the tasks are employees; those who work together to get the job done are co-workers. Like pieces of a puzzle, the players link together to create the whole. Your ability to carry out your part of this picture will enhance your success.

When a workplace player—manager, co-worker, or employee—becomes the central focus of your life, especially if your emotional state is determined by this person's behavior, you are probably in a family relationship trap. When this focus follows you throughout your career, we would doubt that it actually began in the workplace. We would wonder about your family influences and whether it started with a first authority—a parent or early custodial figure. This inappropriate focus does not serve your self-interest; it just interferes with your ability to be effective. Sometimes it also interferes with your ability to see the big picture and your role in it.

If you think you are in a family relationship trap, you need to look at yourself carefully. It is improbable that most of your managers or employees or co-workers have merited the level of personal focus you have been giving them. More likely, you are carrying with you some ghost of the past. Could it have anything to do with prior negative experiences you may have had with authority figures: bosses, teachers or parents? Think about it. Sometimes we have to admit that our current reactions are not based on current reality. Sometimes they reflect our old emotional baggage.

One important attribute of most successful people is their ability to relate effectively and appropriately with other workplace players. They do this regardless of the changes, disappointments, injustices, or pressures that they confront. You can be a winning workplace player. It doesn't matter what position you are playing. Everyone's position is important. Just focus on playing your position well, letting others do the same, and working together as a team—whether you are a manager or an employee. That's what we call being effective. It will also forward your professional self-interest.

The following is an exercise that you may find helpful in breaking out of a family relationship trap.

TRAP BREAKER
....

One Big Family

Answer the questions in the first section to help you identify the problem. Then move on to the questions in the other section or sections that apply to you.

Identifying the Problem

The first step is to identify the relationship problem. Answer the following questions:

1. Write down the things that your manager/employee/co-worker does or does not do that upset you.

   grandstands, interrupts, demands attn

2. Do similar concerns follow you in similar relationships with different people and different jobs?

   No

3. What are the behaviors that upset you in this manager/employee/co-worker?

4. Are certain styles more likely to cause relationship problems for you—for example, disapproving, displaying temper, distant, noncomplimentary, too complimentary?

   phoney

5. Write down any similarities you may have noticed among people with whom you have relationship problems. Are they all of the same gender? Around the same age? Are they members of the same race or ethnic group? Do you see any connection to your past?

Relationship Problems with Your Manager

Challenge your problem relationship with your manager by putting his or her role in perspective. Answer the following questions:

1. What is your manager paid to do?

   Carry mgt's message

2. What pressures is your manager under?

3. Who does your manager report to, and what is that person paid to do?

4. What messages is your manager responsible for conveying to you?

5. What does your manager need? Is there anything you can do to provide these things? Can you see any way in which providing these things might be in your self-interest?

   — Needs to have me do what she ask

6. What do you need from your manager? Which of these needs are in your professional self-interest? Which are strictly personal?

7. What are your manager's strengths and weaknesses? How do your own strengths and weaknesses complement or clash with those of your manager? How can you use your manager's strengths to help you forward your professional self-interest?

8. What does your manager have to offer or teach you? How can you use what your manager has to offer you?

9. What are your professional goals? Is your manager blocking your achievement of those goals? If so, how? How can you overcome your manager's actions?

10. Considering your manager's style, how should you approach him or her in order to get what you want?

11. In what ways is your relationship with your manager too personal? Be specific. (For example: "I am compromising quality in order to impress my manager"; "I am not keeping him informed of anticipated problems because I'm afraid he will be angry with me.")

12. What actions can you take to make sure that you do not get stuck in a personal relationship trap? What do you need to do or learn in order to effectively carry out these actions?

Relationship Problems with Your Co-Workers

Challenge your problem relationships with your co-workers by putting your roles in perspective. Answer the following questions;

1. Do you feel your co-workers unfairly get recognition that you don't get?

2. Do you think your co-workers are too competitive?

3. Do you feel that your co-workers walk over you?

4. Have you been unfairly passed over for a promotion because of the aggressiveness of co-workers?

5. Is there a co-worker whom you try to avoid or spend a lot of time resenting?

Yes

6. Have you ever gotten so angry at a co-worker that you had to temporarily leave work?

Yes, Bace the only

7. Do your feelings about a co-worker or co-workers affect your ability to do your best?

8. Do you trust your co-workers to get their jobs done?

9. Do you and your co-workers ever disagree about how work assignments should be approached? Who typically wins?

10. Has any of your co-workers complained about you to your boss?

11. Have you complained about any of your co-workers to your boss?

12. Have you ever thought about quitting your job or transferring to get away from a co-worker?

13. Have you made career decisions based on what you heard from your co-workers about the future of your company?

    no

14. Have you ever been frightened about your future based on rumors in the workplace?

    yes

Relationship Problems with Your Employees

Challenge your problem relationships with your employees by putting your role in perspective. Answer the following questions:

1. In what ways do you work toward getting the full efforts of all of your team members? Do you give out any messages that there are exceptions to this?

2. In what ways do you act in the role of the company's messenger? (For example: "My team members know they are expected to meet their goals and maintain their job performance.")

3. Have you ever let the relationship between you and one or more of your team members get too personal? Give examples.

4. In what ways have you protected your self-interests as manager? (For example: "For support, I have formed alliances with other managers whose self-interests were similar to mine.")

5. List what you feel to be your responsibilities as manager.

6. List employee expectations or things that you have taken upon yourself that clearly are not your responsibility as manager.

7. How do you deal with an employee who gets angry with you or asks for special consideration? Give examples of how you behaved in a personal manner and in a professional manner.

8. How could you be more clear about your expectations?

9. What could you use to help your team accomplish its goals (for example, motivational techniques, consultation, and training)?

10. List an example of when you mismanaged a team member. Then list tools or techniques you could have used to more effectively manage that person, such as more accurate evaluation, clearer direction, additional skills development, or performance feedback.

More Strategies for Dealing with Personal Traps

To succeed in the workplace, we must take the initiative and be responsible for our own success. Unfortunately, we have seen many people lose their balance and their perspective. In Part 2, we will focus on strategies you can use regardless of the specific trap or situation involved. These are general strategies that will help you become more effective in a variety of situations. We will explore your attitudes, beliefs, and behaviors in the workplace. You will be encouraged to look at your own situations and apply some important principles: managing yourself, increasing your workplace value, maintaining a balanced lifestyle, identifying and networking with allies and mentors, aspiring toward mutuality, and shining your own light.

Chapter 7

Managing Yourself

In our experience as employee assistance professionals, we have seen many employees receive the bad news—layoffs are coming, management will change, downsizing is pending, an acquisition is in the works, your job is on the line. Suddenly it seems as if everyone is working with a danger signal flashing. We hear expressions of shock and panic: What a disaster! I'm finished! I'm ruined! After all I've done, now they screw me! I just bought a house! How will I tell my family? What will I do now?

We have also seen all of the classic signs of stress and tension: fingers tapping, legs swinging involuntarily, red eyes and tight expressions, pacing, and running back and forth to the bathroom. A few days later, a lot of people are taking something for headaches, stomachaches, back pain, or "their nerves." There are sweaty palms and ice-cold fingers. Forgetfulness and lack of concentration seem to be the rule rather than the exception. Depression is all around. Most people are dominated by their fear.

After the first shock wears off, people work under a cloud of doom. They are filled with anger, fear, and tension. For many, these feelings lead to depression and heightened anxiety. The depression causes them to feel tired, sluggish, and "down." The anxiety makes it hard for them to be calm or stay focused. With all this frenetic energy, these people are still expected to produce and act as if nothing has happened. It is apparent that they are on a frightening and hazardous road without a map. The last thing on their mind is doing their job, or rationally planning their next career move.

In such a situation, most people's thoughts are so focused on catastrophe that they cannot really understand and process what they are told. Furthermore, they are unable to focus on what they have to do to deal with their situation. As we watch their reactions it is clear to us that they will have to find a way to manage their "self" during this stressful time.

Bad news can lead to a negative spiral—a barrage of negative thoughts and images. This barrage builds to fear, anger, resentment, and such thoughts of doom as, "We'll lose the house!" "How will we afford food?" "What will people think?" It can also add to feelings of self-doubt and diminished self-esteem. Physical symptoms often follow. This spiral can be broken. But it must first be understood.

Cognitive behavioral therapists and researchers have studied this phenomenon in depth. According to their research, all emotions result from a prior thought. We may not always be aware of the thought, but it is there. We will use an example from a changing workplace.

Before employees find out about the impending changes, they often feel relatively secure and comfortable with their work status. They may be thinking that they can count on keeping their job, or that their career is on track. Even if there are problems, they think they know how to handle them. These thoughts result in positive feelings of satisfaction or happiness, or in neutral feelings, or in boredom.

Once people find out about a downsizing or merger, they immediately think about what that will mean for them. They start thinking about how they will pay their bills, what to do next, and how they will tell people (or themselves) that they are unemployed. This thinking leads to feelings of fear, worry, panic, shame, and despair, which cause the stress and tension that lead to physical symptoms. They often catastrophize, imagining the worst possible outcome.

What would happen if an employee started thinking that the changes might present opportunities for him or her to advance more quickly? Could this same workplace change lead to feelings of hope and excitement and, ultimately, to a positive spiral?

The methods we will discuss in this chapter are all cognitive behavioral approaches that we have adapted to the workplace. As we discuss specific situations in the chapters that follow, we suggest that you refer back to some of the principles and strategies recommended in this chapter. We will show you the many ways in which you can take control.

Managing Anxiety and Stress

We will start with the anxiety and stress associated with the negative spiral. Research shows that anxiety and stress are really the result of adrenaline running out of control. As Herbert Benson shows in his best-selling book *The Relaxation Response,* when we tell ourselves that we are in danger, our body gears up to act. The instinctive response is called *fight or flight*—the primal self-protection response that is programmed into us as human beings. We automatically produce the chemical adrenaline, which is sent throughout our body when our brain says we are in danger. Adrenaline energizes us to take action. It causes the heart to beat faster and the blood pressure to rise.

The positive side of the "adrenaline shower" is that the extra energy can come in handy. For our ancestors, it often meant the difference between life and death. In fact, adrenaline was so necessary to their basic survival that those who did not produce it quickly enough in the face of danger probably did not survive. Their workplace, the natural environment, was extremely dangerous. If a hunting party was attacked by an animal, they had to suddenly produce huge amounts of energy in order to stay alive. That same burst of adrenaline helps us respond to our modern emergencies. It also gives us an extra edge when we are working on an important project, actively involved in sports, or dealing with a complex social situation.

Unfortunately, there are also times when the "adrenaline shower" can cause problems. For instance, when you are told that a major change such as a merger or a downsizing may occur, you may begin to think: Danger ahead! That thought signals adrenaline to flood your system. But it is difficult to function with this extra surge of energy bottled up inside of you. You cannot fight; nor can you flee. You may be standing next to your boss or sitting at your desk, and you cannot act, even though the energy thrust wants you to. You could attack your boss or co-workers. You could also run out of the office and around the block. But this would obviously not be the best course of action to pursue.

However, unless you do something, you are stuck with this adrenaline shower and no place to direct the resulting energy explosion. So you work hard to contain it. This is what causes your heart to beat quickly, your muscles to tense up or ache, your thoughts to race or your mind to go blank, your blood pressure to rise, your chest or temples to feel tight, your eyes to tear up, your hands to get shaky and clammy, and your head to spin.

There are some proven "adrenaline adjusting" techniques that work on and off the job when the pressure is on. We suggest that before using these techniques at work, you practice them at home. We will present several methods so you can figure out the one(s) that work best for you. After you have practiced them at home, you will be ready to try at work those you have found to be effective. By practicing at home you will be using the principle of *desensitization,* which is commonly used in the treatment of many anxieties. In reality what you are doing is stimulating the same body responses that you experience at work and then practicing techniques to control them.

Take a Deep Breath

In *The Relaxation Response,* Benson teaches the benefits of deep diaphragmatic breathing. Deep breathing can help you lower your blood pressure and general stress reaction. Controlling your breathing does this more effectively than many other self-regulating techniques. Just as it can reduce your stress reaction, so can it help you maintain or regain the self-control that is needed during difficult and threatening situations at work. You will be able to think straight and remain in control. The beauty of this technique is in its simplicity. It is something you will always have with you.

Rapid breathing caused by the adrenaline thrust we already talked about robs your body of the oxygen you need to think clearly and make better decisions. It also causes you to exhale too much carbon dioxide, which can lead to feeling light-headed and causes dizziness, shakiness, and heart palpitations that we associate with anxiety. These symptoms get in the way of being effective at your work and can be prevented simply by learning how to breathe with a purpose. Frank Mitchell and Wes Willis (*Relax and Live,* 1997) point out that when we chest-breathe, we use only about 30 to 50 percent of our lung capacity. When we use our stomach to breathe we use 100 percent of our lung capacity. This allows us to get the oxygen into our system that will bring clarity of thought and better decision making.

Obviously, diaphragmatic breathing will not be the answer to all of your problems, but it will help you stay in control of yourself during the situation and not allow the situation to control you. Now try the following exercise.

e x e r c i s e   1

Diaphragmatic Breathing

1. Sit in a quiet place and in a comfortable position with very straight posture. Locate your diaphragm—the soft spot below your rib cage.

2. Practice deep breathing using your stomach instead of your chest. To do this, breathe by moving your diaphragm up and down. Slowly allow your stomach to fill up with air. Then slowly exhale that air through your mouth. Some people find it more effective to breathe in with their mouth closed, and to pucker the lips (as if blowing out a candle) as they slowly exhale. Keep doing this for a while. You may find that you are getting a sensation of mental clarity or bodily exhilaration.

3. Select a word, phrase, or sound that will replace the brain's panicked thoughts with calming ones. One method is to repeat silently a two-syllable word such as "re-lax" or "calm down." Say the first syllable while breathing in, and the second while slowly breathing out.

Practice at home repeating your chosen syllables to yourself while deep breathing. In this way, you are controlling your body and your "self-talk." You also can use any self-talk message that is positive or pleasurable for you and that will control the self-message of disaster, such as *popcorn:* "pop" (air in) "corn" (air out), or *ocean:* "o" (air in) "cean" (air out).

When you are ready, imagine doing this exercise as you are about to face the boss or a dreaded meeting. Don't be surprised if a disaster message tries to creep in, causing your adrenaline to start pumping. Just counter this message by continuing to repeat your chosen syllables. You may recall that this method worked for Elliot, who was stuck in the "My Manager's Out to Get Me" trap, as he was controlling his angry reaction to his manager. It allowed him to manage himself in order to manage the situation.

Daydream

Some "fires" may be too hot to put out with deep breathing alone. Such situations call for an added technique that utilizes something we probably all know how to do—daydreaming, or visualizing a pleasant situation. You have probably done this in a class, listening to a boring lecture, or getting through a tedious meeting. Daydreaming helps us escape a boring situation by mentally taking us to a more pleasant one—for example, a day at the beach, the golf course, or an exotic vacation spot. Visualization is a proven way to cope temporarily with stress and anxiety. It is a way to regain balance so you can face the challenge before you.

Your visualization must be effective enough to protect you from what is happening around you in the workplace. It must calm you down and help you gain control. It must, in a sense, keep whatever is happening around you from touching you until you can calm down. It must create a mental barrier between you and the "hostile force."

As you may recall, Kathryn, who was stuck in the "My Manager's Out to Get Me" trap, had to deal with a very confrontational and critical manager. When she was not in the presence of her manager, she could develop strategies for dealing with him.

But when they were in the same room, Kathryn became tense and frightened, especially when her manager verbally attacked her. So Kathryn imagined being surrounded by a layer of impenetrable cellophane. She could then imagine the manager's words bouncing off of the cellophane and not getting through to her. Remember also Beth, who found herself caught between her angry staff and her demanding managers. She found that an imaginary shield helped her hold onto herself and not be controlled by the fear and anger that were shooting through her body.

Now it's your turn. It will feel silly at first, but as you practice, it will feel more natural.

exercise 2

The Imaginary Shield

1. Sit in a quiet, comfortable place with your eyes closed. Now imagine your shield. It can be transparent, Teflon, bulletproof fiberglass, or anything else that works for you. Cover yourself with the shield.

2. In your mind's eye, see yourself in that awful work situation facing that person who makes your life miserable. Now imagine his or her hurtful words coming at you and hitting the shield before they can get to you.

3. Just watch as the words continue to bounce and slide off, while you become more and more relaxed.

Not all shields are invisible; sometimes they can be seen. We all have observed the way people physically shield themselves. They do this by crossing their legs or arms, putting their hands over their mouth or chin, or rubbing their chin or neck. People who study body language, such as Julius Fast in his book *Body Language in the Workplace,* describe "closed" and "self-protective" behaviors. We know people who only need to put their hands up or in front of their face to feel protected; this is the only shield they need to control the adrenaline thrust. For some people, physical shields are such a natural part of their physical posture that they may not even view them as protective.

Redirect Your Energy

Have you ever felt so out of control and angry that your whole body tingled? If so, deep muscle relaxation may work better than the other techniques we've already discussed. The only problem is that this technique is not as portable as the others are. However, we have adapted it for the workplace so that it need not be so obvious.

The idea is to redirect your energy to a place in your body other than places that will cause you to tense up, or show your discomfort, or cloud your thinking. You probably already practice this energy diversion technique automatically without realizing it. If you find yourself clenching your jaws, pressing your fingers together, pinching yourself, or merely rubbing your chin, you are diverting your energy away from pressured and embarrassing responses such as twitching, blushing, or stuttering. The following exercise shows some techniques you can use.

---

e x e r c i s e   3

Energy Diversion

1. Try diverting some of the "anger energy" from your face to your arm by tightening and loosening your fist. If this is too noticeable, try pushing your thumb and index finger together as hard as you can.

2. Try snapping a rubber band on your wrist to sharply refocus negative energy. It is literally a way to "snap out of it."

3. This technique comes from Daniel Sheehan, in the book *The Anxiety Disease.* He recommends rubbing under the ear lobe. We have found that for different people rubbing the back of the neck, the chin, or other spots relieves tension. We know someone who curls his toes tightly as a way to focus his energy and stay calm. Try it!

Count to Ten

Last but not least, there is the time-honored approach of just slowly counting from one to ten. The idea here is that if you are focused on counting to ten, you are closing out the other adrenaline-producing thoughts. It is simpler than the other techniques we have discussed, yet it is an effective method of diverting your thoughts.

Adjusting Your Thoughts

Research done by cognitive therapists such as Aaron Beck support the idea that the self-talk or messages that you give yourself determine how you feel. You cannot do a job well if you continue to tell yourself that you are stupid or you can't do it. These negative self-messages will divert the energy you need to do a good job.

You have more control over your thoughts than you think. We have met many competent people who tell themselves that they "can't do it" or that they are "not smart enough." These self-critical messages become self-fulfilling prophecies, and they get in their way of doing a good job. Others are preoccupied with the thought that a disaster is about to occur. This thought produces so much tension and anxiety that it diverts the energy they need to do a good job.

We all talk to ourselves from time to time. This self-talk is natural. As we saw before, your self-messages determine how you feel. If you say negative things to yourself, it will cause you to feel negative about your competence. Studies have shown that if you tell yourself you cannot do something, chances are your ability to do it will decrease. At the workplace, this will result in poorer job performance. You must learn to challenge negative messages such as, " I can't do this job," "I'm not going to make it with this new management," or "I'm dead if I make a mistake." These self-messages become traps for many people when they are confronted with the dangers of a changing workplace. We will show you ways to counter those messages.

Stay in the Present

Remember Charles, the hardworking plant manager whose boss became very tough and demanding when the company began to lose money? Suddenly Charles could do nothing right. His negative self-messages were so powerful and compelling that they got in the way of his ability to focus on what he had to do. He was unable to be as creative as he needed to be. His mind was so full of these messages that he had little room to do his job. These danger thoughts caused an adrenaline thrust and energy surge that were hard for him to control.

Our task was to help Charles focus on the job at hand. He needed to focus on getting the job done. His task was to stay in the present and focus on each step, one at a time, that had to be taken to complete the job. He could not afford to think of future doom, nor could he afford to long for the past. Most important, he could not afford an adrenaline thrust that would lead him into a negative spiral. Any thoughts that went beyond his present tasks would only get in his way and divert his energy, and thus sabotage future success.

You must resist the temptation to play that recorder with the doom messages from past experiences. You must challenge messages such as, "The same thing happened on my last job; I know I will be fired again" or "This boss is just like the last one who set me up to fail." The circumstances may be very similar, but by recognizing them, you can work to make the outcome different. You can be in the driver's seat this time. Just remember not to drive while looking in the rear-view mirror.

If you run into a situation that reminds you of a previous disaster, you may be tempted to curse your fate and run for cover. There is another way: Look back to learn, then try a new way. When the going gets tough in the workplace, bad situations happen. Your ability to learn from them and not waste your time bemoaning your fate will help you keep moving forward.

Noah was an engineer who left his firm when he thought management had become unreasonable in its demands. He went to another firm and was pleased with the way it approached projects. Little did he know that his pleasant days were numbered. This "gentler and kinder" firm changed its ways when the market became more competitive. Soon Noah was facing the same "unreasonable demands" he had just left. Needless to say, he thought of the misery he had experienced in his last job and began imagining the same thing happening all over again.

We helped Noah appreciate the advantage of having been in this situation previously. He had experience that could help him in his current situation. If he looked back to learn, he might have some idea of what to expect, what to avoid, and how to handle things differently. Who knows? He might even learn new responses this time. After all, the industry had changed and he had to change with it. He could now turn this crisis into an opportunity.

e x e r c i s e   4

Turning Crisis into Opportunity

Think about a workplace crisis you have gone through, and answer the following questions:

1. What mistakes did you make?

encouraged them / think to vent unpredictedly

2. How might you improve on them?

3. What did /could you learn from this experience?

4. What could you change next time?

5. Did you play the "it ain't fair" tape over and over in your head? Where did it get you? Where could you put your energy instead?

Yes

6. What were the missed opportunities in the experience that you could focus on now?

7. What were the things you did well in the situation?

Choose Your Messages

Keisha was a designer in an emerging dress manufacturing company. She had to create a line of dresses that would compete with designs from some of the established and successful manufacturing companies. In doing this she had to deal with the people in production, sales, and purchasing, as well as with her management. That was a lot to juggle. She told herself that it was too much for her and that she couldn't do it. Furthermore, this was new to her, and she told herself that she didn't know what she was doing and that some of the people she was dealing with could tell.

As we talked with Keisha, it became clear that these self-defeating messages were getting in her way. They made it difficult for her to listen to what people were telling her. She could not hear the positive feedback she received because she was so focused on the not-so-positive, which she interpreted as negative.

Communications specialists have long recognized the power of the negative. They have found that we are more likely to remember negative messages than positive ones. In fact, researchers say that it takes three positive statements to counteract the impact of one negative statement. People who give themselves positive messages perform better than those who focus on messages of incompetence. Keisha needed to challenge her negative messages and recall the positive messages. She needed to be intentional about choosing the messages that she would react to.

Keisha also needed to find a way to work more effectively with others. She had to give positive messages that would be motivational. Her co-workers' motivation would help *her* to succeed. However, she could not count on them to give her the strokes she needed—she had to do that herself. That is how she would get the fuel to keep driving to the end of the project. She could not afford to give that power to anyone else.

Like Keisha, you need to be able to choose the messages that you respond to. An important part of this process is to give yourself positive messages—and *hear* them. You also need to be able to think clearly enough to assess your situation and give yourself positive strokes; you cannot always wait for somebody else to do it.

We are not suggesting that you ignore constructive criticism or the realities of a bad situation. However, think of criticism as constructive and therefore positive. Think of it as an opportunity to learn and to change. Allow yourself to learn and grow. Don't waste your time second-guessing yourself or beating up on yourself for not being perfect. If you find you are telling yourself that you don't know what you are doing, challenge this self-defeating message by reminding yourself of the skills and training that you do have. Use them. If you come upon a stumbling block, do the extra work or put in the effort to learn what you need to in order to overcome it. Successful people learn to hang in there and search for a way to work it out.

Keep Pushing Forward

There is a valuable lesson to be learned from football. No matter how battered and tired, the players measure their effectiveness ten yards at a time. If they get tackled, they get up and push for more yards. They are always looking for an opening. If there is an interception, they have their defensive team working to get the ball back. Any setback is met with another full effort.

When the times are tough in your company, you may feel battered and tired. What you need to do then is recognize that the best you can do is work toward moving forward, look for openings, and salvage losses as best you can. Keep on pushing. Work toward your success one "play" at a time. You also need to temper your enthusiasm about the big gains. This will protect you from overreacting when you have big losses. Just go to work the next day planning to move ahead with another play.

When we met Keisha, she was telling herself that she was defeated and a loser. However, as we looked at her situation more closely, it became clear to us that she was making definite gains. Unfortunately, she couldn't recognize them. She did not know about playing ten yards at a time—she was focused only on the touchdown. She could not see that key people were listening to her and sharing important information with her, and that she herself was becoming better at knowing what information to ask for. These are all real gains that she needed to recognize.

One of the problems of the new workplace is that management keeps moving the goalpost. The solution is to keep moving with it. Of course, mistakes will be made, but once you cross the goal line you get a touchdown. You can enjoy the excitement, but get right back into the game for the next play. Likewise, when you face serious reversals, you continue to enter the field. A gain may mean doing the best you can in a losing situation. The trick is to measure your gains, become empowered by them, and keep giving yourself positive messages as you move forward.

You Have More Control Than You Think

As you can see, you have more control than you think. In fact, it is how you think that gives you the control. Control is the key to successfully managing yourself, and only you can have that control. We hope some of the techniques we have shown you in this chapter for gaining the skill of self-management will help you be more successful in the workplace.

In order to succeed in today's changing workplace, the first step is to take control of the thought–feeling–physical symptom spiral. You need to manage this spiral, and keep it in the positive to neutral position so that you can develop an effective strategy for understanding and handling your situation. Remember, the negative spiral is not inevitable.

Chapter 8

Increasing Your Workplace Value

You have seen how our friends successfully increased their value in the old workplace. Judith progressed from being a generalist, to human resources specialist, to manager, to a candidate for a director's position. Charles worked his way up from assembly line worker, to supervisor, to section manager, to plant manager. Ana progressed from graphic artist positions for various publicists to a position as art director for a magazine. They were all very successful in the old workplace. Then the new workplace descended upon them. Not only did they not see it coming, but they also were not even sure what it was when it hit them. All they knew was that suddenly their value had markedly decreased.

Who would have believed that in such a short time things could change so radically? Ana could not imagine that she would be let go so abruptly from her art director position. She was not prepared to even look for the signs of such a change, much less know what to do when it happened. To add to her shock, she found that the job opportunities in her field had drastically declined since her last job search. She had never thought to keep up with the information regarding her industry and specialty. In only a few short years, the demand for her skills and experience had almost dried up.

As you will recall, Daniel's lack of knowledge of his value almost caused him to self-destruct. How could they cut his commission? He was worth more than that. Why bother to work hard? He was sure that he could do much better if he made a change. He had not realized that commission structures had generally fallen in his field.

In this rapidly changing environment, we need to rethink how we measure our workplace value. If we get valuable training, all we really know is that it is good for now. If we are in a valued position in our company, we know that this is only true in the present situation. If we were offered several positions in a previous job search, it doesn't guarantee that we will get even one offer the next time we look. The only constant is that there is no constant; nothing can be counted on to stay the same. However, often when one door closes, another opens.

There are opportunities in the new workplace. Rapid changes lead to new needs and new openings. There are many people who are prospering in this environment. Some had the right skills at the right time in the right place and worked hard to get there—not much different from the old workplace. The difference today is that the right skills and the right place are quickly and constantly and unpredictably changing. In this chapter, we will discuss some methods you can use to increase your value in this rapidly changing world.

Marketing Yourself

Successful people in the new workplace view their career like any other important product—they do not take its value for granted. They understand that they are only as valuable as they are marketable. Like any other product, they must constantly adjust, repackage, improve upon, and advertise themselves.

To achieve this, successful people also know that they need to be students of their market. They know that their immediate market is their organization or company. They need to keep abreast of the department they are in, the company they are working for, and even the companies that use their services. They must be aware of the type of skills they have, the demand for those skills, new developments that are now being introduced, projected developments, and developments that may replace what they do or make their skills obsolete. Once they have this information, they must work on increasing their workplace value. This in itself requires that they be willing to challenge what they know, find ways to learn new things, and relocate to new work settings.

How Good Are Your Tools?

When you hire someone to perform a service, you like to know that they are using the best and most up-to-date tools. It's the same in the workplace market. Your tools are what you know and how you do what you do. Your pay is based on the current value of your knowledge and skills.

New technologies and skills are continually being developed. Be assured that there is someone somewhere who is trying to find a way to do what you are doing now more effectively, quickly, and inexpensively. If you do not take advantage of new skills and technologies, your colleagues and competitors will.

We know many people in the medical field who spent years developing practices. They had to develop skills that required the expenditure of both time and money. This included attending college and medical school, internships, and, for many, advanced residencies—not to mention the cost of setting up a practice. They had skills that were greatly valued. However, since most clients could only pay for their services through their insurance policies, the value of the skills was, in reality, set by these companies. As long as the insurance companies were willing to pay, the value remained high. But insurers began to limit the types of procedures they would cover and how much they were willing to pay for them, opting to reduce costs. Many physicians had to change their way of practicing and sacrifice their finances. Those who didn't found themselves short on patients to treat.

Our skills are worth only as much as someone is willing to pay for them. Companies will pay for only the latest skills and knowledge. You need to be able to provide them. If you don't, someone else will. If you don't keep up, someone will replace you.

What Are Your Building Blocks?

In this changing environment, our friends are challenged to find alternatives. Our physician friends found several ways to continue, by banding together into group practices, working for larger groups such as hospitals or managed care companies, or forming advocacy groups. Like the physicians, if Ana recognizes that her field is changing in ways that she does not find interesting or no longer likes, she will need to consider alternatives. If Daniel finds that a career in sales is no longer for him, he will need to look into a change. This is easier said than done and not easy to consider—especially when you feel your current field is the only one you know.

For some people, seeing a career development specialist may be among the first steps that they take; others may take this step later in the process. In either case, you have many more skills and interests than you think. We will get you started by showing you some very general ways to find them. It starts with building on what you have.

How do you think Keisha became a successful designer? She was stuck in a secretarial job that she had no interest in. She also had nowhere to go in her company and wasn't particularly interested in its product anyway. She recognized that she had enjoyed her art studies in college and continued to paint as a hobby. She was also interested in fashion and had spent some time in college selling women's clothing. She liked it and she did it well. Keisha wanted to apply this to a career change. She recognized that her interests could be combined in the design field. To get in the door, she took a position as a secretary in a large design house. It was only a matter of time before she got a position as an assistant in the design department. From there, her talents and enthusiasm spoke for themselves. She also consistently made it a point to do as much learning about the field as she could. Keisha did not just happen to come upon this field. She had a foundation that she was building on. It started with her talent and interest in art and continued with her interest in fashion.

How did Daniel go from being a salesman of chemical products to being a computer-training specialist? For starters, he just could not see himself continuing in the chemical products field. He found it particularly hard to remain motivated to do the traveling and the ongoing fielding of complaints from customers and plant operators; this was an aspect of the job that he did not like, nor did he feel he was particularly good at it. Because of this, his performance was falling, and he knew it. His manager was also noticing it. Daniel knew that he had to make a change, but he did not know how to start. This was all he had ever done.

Daniel needed to take inventory of his foundation. He recognized that he had always been good at subjects connected with mathematics and the sciences. With some self-reflection, Daniel noted that he liked abstract thinking. He was also aware that the computer field had opportunities. He decided to look into computer training. He found a training program that would offer him a foundation in various program applications. It was intensive and required that he attend classes four nights a week and all day Saturday for six months. His ability to apply himself to abstract applications served him well as he learned the computer skills. He enjoyed the learning and did very well in his classes. He also kept an eye on the available opportunities.

Daniel noted that the aspect of sales he enjoyed most was the service. He valued the relationships he developed in the companies. He also enjoyed giving presentations. He concluded that he could combine these skills with his computer skills and do computer training. This was perfect preparation. He was able to get his start in a large chemical manufacturing company, where he eventually became a trainer. The following exercise will help you discover what are your career building blocks.

Career Building Blocks

First inventory your skills and interests by answering the following questions. Be as open as you can. Your answers can include technical, artistic, or people interests and skills. They can include any interests and skills you have, from dabbling to highly trained or professional.

1. What did you do well in at school?

2. What did you enjoy in school?

3. What things do you do well now?

4. Are there volunteer or hobby activities that you enjoy or do well?

Using your answers above, make a list of each activity you enjoy or have enjoyed in the past, the particular skills each activity uses, and where these skills could be applied.

Activities	Skills Used	Where Applied
_____	_____	_____
_____	_____	_____
_____	_____	_____
_____	_____	_____

Now look at your lists. Answer the following questions. Use your answers as guidelines for thinking about how you could apply your own personal building blocks to a career.

1. Which of these things do you do well?

2. Which of these things seem to immerse you?

3. Which of these things seem to just come naturally?

4. Which part(s) of yourself goes into these activities that makes it your thing?

How Valuable Are Your Skills?

Sometimes we do things so naturally that we take them for granted. We may not even think about how we do them. Yet there must be steps involved in the process of doing these things. What goes into your getting them done is important. It requires your skills—skills that may be more valuable than you think.

After dealing with the initial shock of his company's unexpected downturn and the resulting changes, Charles began to see the handwriting on the wall and decided to take action. He decided to assess his own workplace value. Charles had been a Boy Scout leader for the last ten years. Most of his time away from work was spent in activities with this group. He took this for granted, never looking at the skills he used to get the job done. In fact, he never considered it a "job" because it was something he loved to do.

When he looked at his Scout activities, he identified many abilities he had never thought of as skills before. He realized that he was a good motivator. He was good at understanding what motivated each young boy. He was also good at using this knowledge to get the boys to do their best. Sometimes he also found his mediation skills invaluable—not only among the boys in the troop, but also in talking with their parents. In many of these instances, he was able to help them problem solve and broaden their understanding of their child's abilities and/or limitations. Teaching the boys how to take a project from the idea stage to completion was easy since that was what he did at work every day. He had never really realized how good he was at relating to the boys until he thought about how often they came to him for advice about personal things. He really liked being able to help them this way. He had always known that he was a good communicator—both verbally and in writing—but he had never given that a second thought until now.

For the first time, Charles started thinking about a different field: Wouldn't it be nice to get paid for doing this kind of work? By assessing his experience with the Boy Scouts, he began to realize the kind of work that he would value and that would utilize his skills. He also tried to think of ways he could couple these skills with his work-related experiences and skills. Instead of trying to identify a field or profession first, we want you, like Charles, to let your skills lead you. We suggest the following exercise.

e x e r c i s e   6

Skills Value

Pull out the classifieds section of your newspaper. Don't worry, you are not looking for a job.

1. Use a removable nontransparent tape to temporarily block out all of the major professional headings in the section.

2. Now go through *each listing*. Use a transparent marker to highlight the skills asked for that match your identified skills.

3. Now go back and uncover the headings. Surprised? You have probably identified jobs in some fields that you never would have

considered. Often ingredients and activities of an effective person are similar in many fields.

4. Now that you have identified a variety of fields requiring your skills, list where most of the opportunities are. (Don't be surprised if you have never even heard of many of them—it's the new workplace!) Now put a check mark next to those fields that have the greatest appeal.

Continuing to Learn

Regardless of whether you want a new start in a new field or different work in your existing field, learning is key to increasing your workplace value. In the new workplace learning is expected to be a continual process. You must learn in order to increase your value in your existing field or to change fields. Keep in mind that you are not starting from scratch—you have your building blocks. But you need to know how far they can take you and what you still need to learn. This is true whether you are happy with the field you are in and want to continue to increase your workplace value within that field, or you want to change fields and use your building blocks as the foundations for this change.

Are You a Student of Your Organization?

Surviving in today's unpredictable, changing workplace is like driving a fast-moving car into unknown territory. You have to be looking ahead and anticipating changes in the terrain. You also have to be properly equipped to successfully deal with the changes.

In order to keep up or get ahead, you will probably need to change your routine. You will need to take inventory of your value every day. This should be as much a part of your routine as brushing your teeth or reading a newspaper. There is no one way to maintain or increase your workplace value. Given how much a part of your life this effort needs to be, you might as well find a way that will work best for you. We can only share some ideas that have worked for successful people with whom we have interacted.

You will recall how Ana was so surprised when she learned she was being let go. Chances are there are things she could have done to predict or prevent this. As a proofreader, she had confined her attention to her current job responsibilities. This included interactions with the magazine publishers and editors. Her boss was supportive of her as long as what she did worked well. Her interactions with him were confined to those related to her assignment. She did not have much other contact with her co-workers—she simply did not have the time. She was always dealing with very difficult deadlines and last-minute changes. Ana had no time to learn about her company and her place in it. After all, she was doing a satisfactory job. She thought that was all that counted—at least that is how she had been taught to think in the old workplace.

Had Ana done what our friend Andrew did, it might have made a big difference for her. You will remember that Andrew was concerned that his fellow administrative assistants were acting to sabotage him. Only when he began to talk with them did he learn about the new workplace and how it had affected his company. He also learned what his co-workers were doing to succeed. It became clear that they were in survival mode, while he was not. It was then that he knew what he had to do.

For Ana, doing her job perfectly was not enough. What good did this do her when there were plans to completely overhaul the magazine? She might have been able to save her job had she been informed about what was happening in her company. She could have joined in with the change effort, worked on broadening her skills, or searched out another place in the company in which she could try to grow. She could have taken time to look elsewhere and to work on an exit strategy.

In a very real sense, part of her job is to remain informed about developments in her company. Whatever she does is for the company, and that is where her value is determined. Her designs will not mean anything if they do not fit with the magazine's direction. Furthermore, her company is in the position to decide whether to change the magazine concept or discontinue it altogether. Her value would then be measured by her fit with the new plans. If the company made a decision to clean house, her value would be only as a reassigned or former employee.

Part of your job, then, is to make sure that you are informed about the developments in your company. Think of this as your private survival strategy. Sometimes, however, it makes no difference what you do or at what level you function. There may be little you can do if the company no longer supports or endorses your value. It also makes no difference how important or irreplaceable you think you are. Don't forget, the managers who tell you that you are irreplaceable may themselves be replaced tomorrow.

The sooner you get the information you need, the sooner you can begin to take action to forward your self-interest. You need to be a student of your organization. There are several methods for doing this:

☑ Read all company materials and look for relevant information, including changes in staffing, service, and product emphases, geographic priorities, new management, resignations, and financial considerations.

☑ Read material that is written about your company. This could include articles in professional journals and business periodicals, and reviews by financial institutions and analysts. How is the company's stock doing and why? Is there a new product that will threaten what you are working on? Is there a tough competitor entering? Is your management team in trouble? Is there a takeover (hostile or friendly) or merger afoot?

☑ Routinely talk with people who might be in the know or in the loop. Have informal discussions with well-placed administrative folk, management, and people who take pride in being "in the know." Meet them for lunch, at a coffee break, or for coffee after work.

☑ Find out where the changes are occurring. Who is leaving? Are many in-the-know people leaving your area or division? Why are they removing so many resources from this department? Who is that equipment designed to replace? What is the new manager looking for and doing away with?

There are critical questions to ask yourself as you are learning about your company: What potential impact will the information you have gained have on you? On your office? Your department? Your profession? Your location? Once you have answered these questions you will be ready to take action:

☑ If the action is moving elsewhere in your company, you can begin to try to position yourself to get there.

☑ If the company is emphasizing or seems to value skills that you don't have, begin an aggressive strategy to acquire them.

☑ If there appears to be a major shift afoot that could have severe consequences, you need to focus on getting the latest news. Simultaneously, you may want to consider intensifying a search outside the company.

Don't forget that this is a process. Make it a point to continue seeing yourself as a student who is forever a learner and open to new ideas. This means being ready to find new information that contradicts what you learned yesterday. It also means trying things, keeping your eyes open along the way, and being ready to change direction if necessary.

Are You a Student of Your Field?

As we mentioned, you need to be sure that you, "the product," continue to increase your value. This includes keeping up on the latest methods and skills. It also includes being a predictor and staying ahead of the skills/knowledge curve. After all, your skills and knowledge are what you have to offer. They are your product.

Part of your job, then, is to be a student of your field. It is to find out the newest developments and the latest trends. You will need to do this to protect yourself as a professional. This transcends your current position or your current company. It will be what you have to offer any future employer. It is what you will have to market. There are several ways of doing this:

☑ Make it a point to regularly read your professional journals.

☑ Attend meetings of your professional association—especially those related to new developments.

☑ Keep informed of your alumni association's activities—especially those related to your career area.

☑ Maintain contact with a network of people who are on top of your field and its developments. More active involvement in committees in the above organizations could be one way of doing this. Other, more informal arrangements will also work.

☑ Pursue new developments by attending professional seminars, conferences, continuing education programs, and relevant courses. An investment in travel to get intensive training in such an area may be worth considering.

We again emphasize that this is an ongoing process.

Are You Prepared to Make a Change?

How do you proceed if your research suggests that you pursue a new field? The first step is to look at your building blocks and appreciate that you have many experiences and strengths that you can build upon now. You may want to consider that making a change in fields is also a process. The earlier you determine this, the more time you will have to prepare. This preparation time is crucial.

You must cherish and apply yourself to what you are doing now. This is the base that you can use while you are looking into finding a new field. But you also need to allow yourself the time for discovery and focus.

After you have completed Exercise 6 using the classifieds, move on to the following exercise.

e x e r c i s e 7

Preparing for a Change

Go back through each of the listings under the headings you checked in the previous exercise. Study them for qualifications or skills that are listed but that you do not *have. List these below.*

1.

2.

3.

4.

Once you have determined what skills you need to work on, you may want to consider enlisting some outside help. If you have the right allies and mentors (see Chapter 10 for more on this), they can help you start your exploration. You may want to consult a credible professional career service agency. Here are some suggestions on how to do this:

☑ Contact a local high school, college, or university. If they do not offer counseling services, they may track the credible ones. Often such services are offered free for alumni and are available for a fee to the general public.
☑ Contact one of your professional associations.
☑ Seek advice from a trusted colleague.

If you contact a career consultant, be sure to check for proper credentials. This may include checking with accrediting organizations and the appropriate trade or business bureau for any information about him or her.

If you decide you need to acquire additional skills, a referred resource is usually best. Start with accredited colleges and universities, institutes, and training schools that offer such training. Be sure to investigate before you begin. Talk to alumni, credible sources in the field, and/or potential employers. Ask yourself these important questions before you begin training:

☑ What will you have at the end?
☑ Will it be valued in your field?

Following the Path of Workplace Success

Welcome to the new workplace. In order to be successful here, you must become a "marketable product." You must also apply yourself to learning and improving on how to learn. This must become a part of your own personal job description—something that you think about just as you do any other part of your job. Never be satisfied with your current value. Increasing your workplace value must be a daily pursuit. Of course, you can expect some difficulties along the way and may need help at those times. We suggest that you refer to Chapter 10 and marshal some "allies" and "mentors" for this kind of help if you need it. If you stay informed and take action as needed, you will be following the path of workplace success.

Chapter 9

Maintaining a Balanced Lifestyle

Maintaining a balanced lifestyle has never been so important as in today's changing workplace. Employees are quickly being thrust from the familiar old workplace into this unfamiliar and unpredictable new one, shaking their self-worth, self-esteem, and support. They are finding it increasingly difficult to turn off the mounting tension and fear and leave it at the company door. It stays with them in their thoughts and preoccupies them throughout the day, into the evenings, and during the weekends.

In Chapter 7 we discussed how what we think determines how we feel. Preoccupation with negative thoughts about what is going on will produce the negative feelings of anger, frustration, despair, fear, and bitterness. We also discussed how negative feelings cause body tension and distress, and how this negative spiral builds on itself.

The events of work can invade and change your personal world. It is as though your work life and your personal life are both being restructured. In this situation, negative energy can flood into and take over your personal space. In this chapter, we will discuss some ways in which you can work on getting rid of this negative energy and improving the balance between your work and personal life.

Protecting Your Personal Space

Aaron was a trader for a money management firm. He liked his work, worked hard, and functioned well under pressure. He also put a great deal of energy into the "play" part of his life. He and his wife had a good partnership, and they enjoyed their personal life. When Aaron's firm was downsized, he managed to keep his job. However, the reduction in staff and constant changes in expectations from management put a tremendous amount of pressure on him. He also saw himself fighting for a job that seemed uncertain. Each new layoff caused another panic. He was never sure whether he would be the next to go. He began spending much more time at work and brought home a great deal of work.

Aaron was constantly preoccupied with distressing thoughts about his plight. These thoughts caused him to feel scared, angry, and overwhelmed. Nothing seemed to be fun. Work grief followed him everywhere, and he went from misery at work to misery at home and then back to work. Each tension built on another. His body was like a pressure cooker. The pressure built up at work and continued outside of work as he relived his misery. After a while, Aaron was unable to find pleasure in the activities that he and his wife had enjoyed together. That is when he began to have chest pains.

Aaron had negative stress at work that built throughout his day. When he left he took this stress into his personal space. He also gravitated toward other people experiencing the same thing, which only added to his negative thinking. When he returned to work the next day he started with the buildup of the previous day's distress, from both work and home.

Protecting and maintaining his personal space was Aaron's responsibility. Unlike the workplace, he was the boss in his own personal life space. There he was accountable to himself and to those with whom he shared this personal time—his friends and family. He needed to have a strategy to keep the workplace away.

Aaron began to keep a daily journal to help him bring closure to his work state of mind while going to his personal life, and vice versa. He attempted to focus his daily entries on things that he completed or things that he did well. This moved him in the direction of recognizing achievements and celebrating them. No matter how small, he patted himself on the back for a job well done. When he was preoccupied with unfinished business, he wrote a "to do" list or a brief plan to address it, then reminded himself that this business was closed for the day. Then he told himself that work was behind him and he was about to enter his personal world.

Transitioning from Work to Home

Do you recall Will, the hospital administrator from Chapter 4, who was stuck in the "Work Is My Life" trap? Although he had a family, he spent little time with them. Will could only manage to put his energy into work—it was everything in his life. When Will's position was restructured, resulting in a severe reduction of his responsibilities, he described the feeling as "a hole in his soul." To ease the pain, Will began to drink.

Will started out by stopping at a bar with a co-worker on the way home from work to share the misery of the day over a couple of glasses of wine. This seemed to calm him down enough so he could go home. Then as time passed and pressure built up, he needed more wine to get that calm feeling. What he did not know was that after a few hours the effect of the alcohol *increased* his depression, anxiety, and tension—the very feelings he was trying to escape. By the time he arrived home, he felt worse than before he had started drinking. He began to take it out on his family. To make matters worse, he was not even aware that this was happening. He was so preoccupied with being the victim at work that he saw himself as the victim at home as well. With the increased tension at home, he began to stop at the bar more frequently, often alone.

Will's goal of turning down the tension level on the way home made sense. Unfortunately, he was doing it in a way that actually had the opposite effect. This is true for many of the "quick fix" methods people use to deal with work pressures. Alcohol, drugs, and even overuse of sugar can add to the very tensions they are trying to alleviate. They all have side effects that include mood fluctuations, anxiety, irritability, and depression.

Many people feel powerless and use such substances because they believe they cannot deal with the situation on their own. This becomes a self-fulfilling prophecy. It was that way for Will. He convinced himself that the only antidote for his misery and personal pain at work was the calming effect of the alcohol. At the end of the day he told himself, "I need a drink! I earned it!"

Instead of using Will's approach, we suggest that you find a way to use your trip home to slow down the negative energy in your mind and your body. Do it in a way that will empower you. By the time you reach home you will have really left work behind or at least reduced its power over you. The goal is to take back your personal space.

Making this switch can be difficult. As you have seen, the stresses of your work space can easily run into your personal space. You can use methods that will prevent this from happening. We call the methods of successfully moving from work space to personal space *transitional strategies.* We'll share some of them with you.

Your transition is the time that you spend mentally changing from your work life to a focus on your personal life. A filter that separates the two worlds and purifies out the polluted thoughts and feelings is what you need. This leaves space for more positive thoughts and feelings. Let's take a look at some things people have used to filter their worlds.

exercise 8

Transitional Strategies

- If you are driving, take a few minutes in the car before you start the ignition to practice this exercise. (Caution: It's important not to do this or any other meditation exercise while you are driving.)

Think about a running stream. This is the time when you are "floating" from the tension of work to the realm of your personal world. The object is to stop the distressing thoughts and feelings of work from flowing into your personal world.

- If it is still daylight, stop at a relaxing spot on the way home, such as a park, and focus on the beauty around you. Think of positive associations that come up for you. You can also try deep breathing to slow things down (see Chapter 7 for deep breathing techniques).

- Debrief with co-workers in the company cafeteria, a café, or another spot not associated directly with working. This is not to be used as a complaint and misery session—which would only enhance the negativity. Remember that the purpose is to shine positive light on the rest of your day. It will shift your energy. Make the debriefing an opportunity to talk about something other than work. It could be a discussion on how to cope. We hope it will involve humor—smiling will make you feel better, and laughter is a great release.

- If you are taking public transportation, play a tape on a personal cassette player that is relaxing or comforting. Allow your mind to meld into the contents of the tape. Try to focus on the positives in your life. Imagine activities that you enjoy. You can also deep breathe, meditate, or read positive material.

- Work out or go to a gym between work and home. Exercise will help you shift your energy and feel better. Be conscious of the positives and how good it is to be working out. Connect with people you see. Do not allow your work thoughts to invade this space. It will add to your aggression and further diminish your pleasure and your power.

Work on making your home truly a "home sweet home." When you have not transitioned, you end up bringing the negative work energy with you. Everyone is better served if you transform the negative energy of the workday into something positive. If you still have some of the negative energy as you enter your personal world you can try any of the following: Depending upon what reduces your stress, you can jog, take a warm bath, meditate, deep breathe, take a walk, or do whatever works. Don't forget the goal is to transform your energy and your focus. After all, once you get home your family will need your attention. But they need your positive energy, not the negative. If you need more transition time, just explain to your family or roommate that you need additional time to unwind. You can make it up to them once your transition is complete.

Seeking Gratification

To maintain a balanced lifestyle, it is important to work on protecting the things that give you pleasure. These are what we call *gratifiers*. They might include pleasant conversation; involvement in an enjoyable activity alone or with others; working on routines or chores that keep your personal world going; and involvement in civic, spiritual, or other growth-oriented activities. They are your tools for combating the stressors of the new workplace. They can protect you from the stress buildup at work and provide balance. Experiencing gratification *off* the job actually helps *on* the job.

Gratifiers are different for different people. Some people experience a lot of gratification from feeling relaxed. As we have demonstrated, deep breathing and meditation work for many people. You can learn to meditate through various classes and books. Another form of gratification for some people comes from spending time with people who are positive and supportive—people with whom they do not feel they have to be on guard. Others relax with a good book or a favorite hobby. Community service, membership in a social club, and physical exercise do the trick for many.

Many people find that a spiritual understanding centers their thinking. It allows them to view work as part of something that is much larger and far more important. It also offers a faith in an order that transcends the challenges of the workplace and puts them into perspective. Many people turn to this understanding during times of crisis. Just as you can utilize any of the techniques above, you may want to draw on your spiritual dimension as you weigh the importance of what is happening at work. Your workplace may also have clusters of co-workers who are meeting during lunch breaks to reinforce the spiritual dimension in their lives. There are thousands of such meetings in many workplaces. If such an experience helps you refocus your thinking, it could be another tool to help bring balance to your life.

Will directed his workaholism toward identifying and using his personal gratifiers. He was able to identify personal gratifiers that revolved around his family and activities outside of work. His positive energy was reflected in immediate benefits for Will and his family. It demonstrated a healthier lifestyle for his children to emulate. It also made him less dependent on his job for his life's meaning. As you saw, for Will, this had led to disaster. It also resulted in tunnel vision, which made it difficult for him to view his work life realistically. His new balanced lifestyle is also preparing him for what would otherwise be a very difficult retirement. Negative energy has turned positive, and Will has begun to find new meaning in his personal life.

If you have become overpowered by your intense involvement in work and other stressful obligations and chores, you are probably, at best, sporadic in gratifying yourself. Perhaps you have never taken care of yourself in that way. If the stresses at work have gotten in the way of your gratifiers, we recommend that you make a conscious effort to hunt for them. The following exercise will help you.

e x e r c i s e   9

Identifying Your Personal Gratifiers

List the activities in your life that have gratified you in the past. Write down anything that comes to mind without censoring or rationalizing.

I wish I still had time to...

1.

2.

3.

4.

5.

6.

Now take some time to think of things you always wanted to do but never got around to doing. Maybe it was cooking lessons, exercise or yoga classes, piano lessons, dancing lessons, volunteer work, or gardening. Could any of these make sense for you now? Of course, some will depend on specifics: the season of the year, whether or not you want to invest in getting a piano, or whether the cooking class is offered now. Make a "now" list and a "future" list.

Current Gratifiers	Future Gratifiers
1.	1.
2.	2.
3.	3.
4.	4.
5.	5.

Now look at all of your lists and put them in order of practicality.

Gratifiers in Order

1.
2.
3.
4.
5.
6.
7.
8.
9.
10.

Now is the time to get active. For starters, you will need to locate where these activities are offered. That probably will not be as hard as you think. Begin by looking in your immediate community. Most neighborhoods have a community center, a YWCA and YMCA, a community college, and places of worship. Check their newsletters and the local newspapers.

Many people find that religious and spiritual pursuits uplift them and provide a needed balance. If you enjoy being with people but find that your work life prevents you from keeping in touch, renew some of those acquaintances and engage in activities that will get you in contact with people. Don't forget family-oriented gratifiers. Remember that the goal is to have a personal life that has more positive energy.

Halting the Invasion of Negative Energy

It is not enough to identify and engage your gratifiers. You will also need to be prepared to handle the invasion of negative energy that will appear from time to time. It is important to identify when this negative energy invasion is most likely to occur. Do you notice any patterns? The negative energy may be so automatic that you cannot see any patterns. Become conscious of this. It might help to just write down where and when this occurs. You may find that it occurs at the same time each day or night. It may also occur at about the same time each week or month. Some people describe Sunday nights as particularly difficult. It may also occur when you are talking to certain people about particular topics. For some, discussion of things they cannot afford or the great successes of peers can be such a trigger. In knowing this, you can see that what captures so much of your energy is predictable.

The next step is to have a plan. Be prepared to counterattack a negative energy invasion with a strong gratifier. For instance, Aaron knew that around two hours before going to bed he sometimes had an invasion of negative thoughts, so he routinely kept a good book at his bedside. It not only served as a distraction, but it was also very gratifying. He also made it a point not to have any work-related material in his bedroom—only a pad to write down his "to do" list. This allowed him to clear away the clutter from his mind. He added pleasant pictures and objects in his bedroom to set the right mood.

We are realistic enough to know that there are times you may have to bring work home. The consequences of not completing an assignment might lead to real dues paying that you would face the next day. Try not to let this work interfere with your personal space. We know people who will wake up an hour or two earlier to get the work done or do the work after they have had a good dose of uninterrupted personal space.

Reversing the Transition

We have dealt with making the transition from work to home. What happens to our friends as they transition back to work? Aaron's stress level built as thoughts of work began to dominate his mind. His transition back to work started about two hours before he went to bed at night. That is when he would begin to worry about what might happen the next day. He would imagine all kinds of disastrous scenarios as he recalled previous unpleasant situations. On weekends, his miserable thoughts of the following work week began on Sunday afternoon. By that evening, he would be filled with tension. Needless to say, the next morning Aaron was filled with dread. His conversation with his family was brief and negative. The negative energy started before he got into his car. The closer he got to work the worse it became. By the time he walked into work he was overwhelmed with fear and feelings of helplessness. He walked into his office with negativity and tension. This is the only way that he knew, so it seemed normal to him. Because he expected a lousy day, he started preparing himself for it.

We encouraged Aaron to be open to another idea. First of all, he had to realize he had more control than he thought. He could make different choices. He had power. It was important for Aaron to recognize that he could actually feel better and go to work with a more positive start and a lowered tension level.

Aaron worked on actively controlling the stress in his body by exercising before work. First he consulted his physician to be sure that there were no medical concerns. He purchased a stationary bicycle and worked on some simple stretches followed by a gradual increase of time on the stationary bicycle. This resulted in an immediate benefit that he could see and feel. The exercise released negative energy and the accumulated lactates from his joints. He began to experience a "natural high" as a result of a release of the body's natural positive feeling producers, endorphins. Eventually he increased his exercise regime and actually woke up looking forward to exercising. He found that he was starting his workday with less tension, a more positive attitude, and a feeling of being more in control. His co-workers wondered what had come over him.

Some people use an exercise specialist or join a gym in order to get additional guidance and motivational coaching. Some prefer to exercise outdoors, hoping that the scenery will hold their interest. The important thing is that you see the benefit and do not get bored.

Also beneficial are activities that direct the thinking in a positive or empowering direction. Many people benefit by starting their day meditating, reading daily affirmations (there are many such books available in the self-help section of your bookstore), or listening to affirming or relaxing audiotapes.

You can prepare for work-related stress by getting your body and mind ready for the rigors of the day. For Aaron, it was paying off. The positive result of the balance between his work life and his personal life had spilled over into the workplace.

Changing your perspective is key to holding on to these changes. Think of work as the means by which you are able to afford and enjoy your personal life, rather than as an end unto itself. This is something you may need to keep telling yourself, rather than thinking about what's wrong about work. Think of ways to win and succeed. Think in terms of action that you can take to better forward your self-interest, both at work and away from work. It is your responsibility to take care of yourself. That is one of the rules of the new workplace.

Valuing Others Who Share
Your Personal Space

Remember Justine, who was stuck in the "They Can't Do This to Me" trap? Her work with a nationwide healthcare company was the center of her life. That life was shattered when the company downsized and demoted her. The pressure at work became unbearable for her. To make matters worse, she became very critical of her husband. He could never seem to bring home enough money or do enough around the house. The stress followed Justine from work to home and to work again. Her gratification from work was gone, and she had not developed any personal gratifiers. She had no break from the negative energy. Eventually she was overcome by a depression that made it impossible for her to function in either place. It nearly destroyed her marriage.

Valuing the others who share your personal space is important. If there is a problem in a personal relationship, it needs to be addressed. Using work as a distraction will only make it worse. If either of you is the target of the other's displaced anger and stress, then both of you need to deal with it.

Establishing a balanced lifestyle requires that you both nurture and be nurtured. Being nurtured is probably one of the best ways to cope with stress. Let others nurture you. It will feel good and move your own psychic and physical energy in a positive direction. Keep in mind that no one wants to nurture a grouch. Therefore, as you nurture it will be easier to receive it in return. Balance is important here also. Nurturing cannot be unilateral. You must get something from it and give something to it. You can teach your family how to change and how to help you change, and you will all feel better for it. Here are some guidelines:

☑ *Communicate.* Sit down with your partner (or other personal space sharer) and state the problem as you see it. Be clear about how what is happening is impacting you and your ability to function. Listen to your partner. The book *Your Perfect Right* by Robert Alberti and Michael Emmons is a useful resource that may help you with this.

☑ *Take corrective action.* Once you have identified and presented what you see as the problem, the next step is to do something about it. This could involve having ongoing problem-solving discussions, reading self-help books, or seeking professional counseling.

☑ *Find shared personal gratifiers.* Do not let your gratifier become a distraction that allows you to avoid the relationship problem and the accompanying alienation and hostility in the household. If used that way, gratifiers will only divert you from appropriately addressing the problem. Justine's short-term remedy for her marital problems was to acquire a group of positive friends to become her gratifiers. While it was a gratifier, it also reduced her investment in repairing or ending the marriage. Justine eventually began to spend more time finding and doing things that she and her husband could enjoy together. Shared personal gratifiers can help to facilitate a strong relationship bond.

☑ *Listen.* Ask questions to learn where family members are coming from and listen for what they need.

☑ *Ask for feedback.* Ask them how they think things are going in their outside lives and what are their perceptions about the dynamics of the family life. Be just as accountable to your family members as you are to your manager. If you promise to change they should hold you accountable, and you should hold yourself to your word.

☑ *Allot quality time to your family members.* Plan activities and relaxation time.

☑ *Do your (office) homework on your own time.* Do not impose your work on family time.

If you follow these rules, you will be able to successfully balance your work and personal life. Don't forget your family will be there well after your work is gone.

Keeping the Positive Energy Flow

Your energy will flow from work to your personal space and back again. You are in a position to keep that flow as positive as possible. If you do nothing, the power of the negativity of work will flow into your personal space. If this happens, you will undoubtedly pay a high price. You can prevent the negative flow from work from entering your personal life by having the positive energy from your personal life flow back into your work space. Find several methods and make them work for you. Some of the techniques we discussed in Chapter 7 may be helpful, both at home and at work.

Contrary to how you may feel, there are more resources available to you today than ever before, and it is important that you use them. Your talents and skills alone are not enough. To succeed, you need the help of others.

Chapter 10

Marshaling Your Allies and Mentors

If you want to succeed in the new workplace, you cannot do it alone. You need others in your corner—not just any others, but special others. You are dealing with a world fraught with pressures, big stakes, surprises, and changes. Going back to our previous sports analogy, the new workplace can be compared to the world that football players confront. Yet, even the most talented football players have all sorts of people in their corner supporting, challenging, and advising them. Their special people are their coaches, managers, teammates, and even fans. Your special people are your allies and mentors.

Allies and mentors are both sources of support, but they serve different purposes. With an ally, you gain sustenance and support. You relax and have fun, you are able to refresh yourself, receive assurance and support, and feel connected and cared about. With a mentor, you are being challenged, solving problems, making decisions, taking action, monitoring results, and continually developing strategies that are key to your self-interest. You will need to learn how to identify and interact with both of these networks of insiders. We will help you to do this, using our human resources manager, Judith, as an example.

Judith had devoted her life to her company and to its president—whom she was sure was equally devoted to her. After the restructuring, she was certain that the newly formed director position would be hers as promised. The announcement came from the president at a staff meeting: The new position of director of the human resources department was to be filled from the outside.

Judith was in shock. She was further insulted and hurt because she had not been told in private about the appointment. Nor had she been given a chance to interview for it. Her reaction only worsened with time, as she saw that the new director was very tough and had a no-nonsense way of treating employees. This approach was totally alien to her. She felt that it was destroying the positive relationships she had worked to maintain with her employees through the years.

Judith bitterly disliked the new director and let him know it. Sometimes she made it a point to show him up in front of other employees. She also let him know what she thought about his management style. He responded by holding closed staff meetings that did not include her—which infuriated her even more.

The personal rage built to the point that Judith felt she could hardly bear it anymore. She felt she had to go over the director's head. She would speak with her "friend" the president, whom she thought would understand her position. In her desperation, she forgot that this "friend" had gone back on his "promise" to promote her. She wanted to convince him that he had made a mistake in hiring this "monster."

You saw what happened. Although Judith's "old friend" was polite, he told her that she would have to register all of her complaints with her new manager. He also added that her new director appeared to be doing a good job. How could she have been so naïve? You will recall that the next day her new director mentioned that he was aware that she had talked with the president. He also requested that she register her complaints directly with him. Within a few weeks, she was told that her office was being moved to the far corner of the department and she found herself flooded with a great deal of paperwork. Now she felt really trapped.

In contrast to management, which had formulated a plan with the help of specialists and consultants, Judith was on her own in the middle of all of these major challenges. Their staff included a manager to execute the human relations part of the plan. Management had the power to call all of the shots, whereas Judith felt she could only react. At the same time, she was being pressured to complete difficult work assignments. She saw herself as powerless, outnumbered, and isolated. She was confused and overwhelmed.

Judith had every reason to do what she did. She felt betrayed, insulted, demeaned, and disrespected. She was watching her efforts go for naught as her department was becoming more callous and cruel to the employees with whom she so identified. All of these *personal* assaults became unbearable. She reacted, yet every action she took seemed to make matters worse. Her entire career and all that she believed were being turned upside down.

Contrary to how she felt, Judith was not alone. She had many people in her personal life who played an important part in how she felt and behaved. For Judith, this was a time to mix personal and work life. In this chapter, we will look at the impact of these personal influences—our allies and mentors—on our personal and work lives.

Allies: Our Attitude Adjusters

Judith did not get to where she is without having people who supported her. In the more predictable, familiar, and friendly old workplace, she had a support network that she valued and welcomed. They were her allies. These included her family and special friends. As she was experiencing this new workplace crisis, her allies not only listened to her and saw her pain, but they also sympathized with her and supported her point of view.

Allies serve a very important role: They are the people who are on our side. The operant conditioning of psychologist B. F. Skinner demonstrates that people who are rewarded with encouragement and support for performing well perform better than those not rewarded for doing so. In order to have a better chance at success, you need to have people who are on your side—people who believe in you. Such unconditional support and validation offer a needed spiritual and self-confidence boost.

In a workplace filled with uncertainty, confusing feedback, and constant evaluations of your worth, your allies can offer you a big part of the balance we discussed in Chapter 9. They can listen, show concern, and be in your corner. They provide the fuel that will keep you going. Utilizing what your allies have to offer is to your advantage.

Engaging Your Allies

Potential allies surround your life. You know them in their roles as family members, friends, neighbors, co-workers, and classmates. But how do you engage them as allies? Bear in mind that your objective is to form a bond based on mutual concern, support, and respect. It has to go both ways.

Begin by focusing on their lives. Include them in your life by telling them about how and what you are doing. You cannot just wait for this to happen—you need to consciously engage your allies. It helps if you have common interests that you can share. There has to be give and take. Mostly, it requires an understanding and continued development. Having effective allies who resist the temptation to mentor is tricky. They will need help. You need to tell your allies what is helpful and what is not. The guide in Chart Two provides some helpful hints.

Feel free to show your allies this guide. They certainly want to be helpful. Just as you may not be clear about how you are coming across, your allies may be equally unaware. You can also use it as your own guide as you take on the ally role with others.

Becoming Your Allies' Ally

We meet many people whose actions cause them to lose out on the support and encouragement that their allies could give them. Remember Tony, for example, who was stuck in the "I'm Mad and

chart two
Guide for Allies

Effective Allies	Ineffective Allies
Listen	Impose their opinions
Are supportive	Tell you what to do
Share time	Judge your actions and feelings
Share activities	Impose expectations
Are available	Withdraw
Acknowledge when you are hurting	Disapprove
Help you take care of yourself	Do most of the talking

I Don't Care Who Knows It" trap? He eventually learned to control his openly expressed anger at work by using the "poker player's" strategy. But at home it was another story.

Tony's wife and children had learned to expect the daily onslaught. Tony would come home each day in a foul mood. He always had the same complaints about work. He would yell about how his manager was always treating him unfairly, criticizing him, and never giving him credit for his work. He complained about how no one could be trusted any more. He would then go on about his fears about his future in the company—a company that no longer valued him.

The entire family had to brace themselves for Tony. They would start preparing before he came home. They would sit through a miserable dinner, and brace themselves for his reaction if anyone crossed him. When the children encountered a misfortune, Tony would lecture them about the horrors of the world and how they had to prepare themselves for it. He became just as critical and demanding of his children as he said his manager was of him.

The family didn't realize it, but they were mirroring Tony's moods. If Tony came home totally wiped out, withdrawn, and sulking, that became the mood of the family. Both Tony and his family were miserable. They were living the negative energy that was overwhelming him. Unfortunately, Tony was also being a negative role model to his kids for how to deal with their own stressors.

Rather than striving for the balance of positive energy that we discussed in Chapter 9, Tony was increasing his stress level. This caused him to bring even more stress to his work the next day, adding to the negative spiral. Tony was also burdening his family with stress and negativity, and their negative response was, in turn, adding to his negative spiral. Tony might not have been aware of how he was affecting his family. Often our behaviors are automatic. This is particularly true when we are under stress. The "safe" people in our lives become the easiest targets for our frustration. Tony was acting out of frustration, and his family was an easy target. He was not helping them.

You can help your loved ones become your allies. They can help you find balance in today's changing world, but you may need to help them. The following assessment will help you become more aware of your own frustration levels and how positive your interactions with your family are.

---

assessment two

Ally Awareness Checklist

The answers to these questions will go a long way toward helping you determine whether your interactions with your family and other allies are what they should be.

Frustration Level Awareness

	True	False
1. I am usually angry about something at work.	____	____
2. I spend most of the time with my family and friends complaining and being negative.	____	____
3. I am usually more critical and judgmental of my family during this time.	____	____
4. I find myself withdrawing.	____	____
5. I impose my views onto my family.	____	____

	True	False

6. I have difficulty listening to my family and friends. ____ ____

7. My family members are generally quieter than usual around me during this time. ____ ____

8. Often my family members seem angry during this time. ____ ____

If you answered "True" to any of these questions, your frustration level may be higher than you are aware.

Positive Interaction Awareness

	True	False

1. I rely on my family and close friends for sustenance. ____ ____

2. I listen for their view of things. ____ ____

3. I feel positive energy when I am with them. ____ ____

4. There is positive interaction when I am with them. ____ ____

5. My friends and family members openly share their own experiences and concerns with me. ____ ____

If you answered "False" to any of these questions, your interaction with your allies may not be as positive as it could be.

If you are not aware of whether your ally interaction is positive, here are some questions you can ask them:

- ☑ Do I bring tension home?
- ☑ Do I seem angry or demanding?
- ☑ Do I carry on about my job?
- ☑ Am I withdrawing?
- ☑ Am I difficult?
- ☑ Am I extraordinarily judgmental?
- ☑ Do you have a difficult time talking with me?

Remember that if you ask the questions, you need to be prepared to hear the answers. Listen and absorb the feedback you get. Share your desire to correct these patterns and find ways to do this.

Understanding the Role of an Ally

We all have people who influence us. They influence what we do and how we feel. They include people who are close family, friends, and special co-workers. They can be people we talk with regularly, such as neighbors and fellow commuters. Our clergy, teachers, lecturers, and counselors influence us, and let's not forget characters in books, on television, and in the movies, and even authors of self-help books.

Your allies include all of those people in your life who sacrificed for this moment, those who will be materially hurt because of this thing that is happening in your life. It includes peers who will clearly have less respect for you if you do something that they do not approve of. It includes the images of successful people that you feel you no longer measure up to.

Sometimes our allies impose their views on us. Many people will tell you what to think and feel. They may even criticize you for reacting as you do. Some will tell you what they did. Some will tell you what they didn't do and still regret. Some will even tell you what to do. Sometimes their influence is subtle, as in the case of the family member who is personally disappointed or hurt, or that of a child who watches his or her parent accepting being demeaned.

In general, Judith's allies did not know enough about her workplace to help her understand what was happening around her or what to do. Even if they had had the information, they would have had to be careful not to allow their personal feelings to color their ability to objectively evaluate her very complex work situation.

Judith's well-meaning allies gave her feedback and advice that was not in her best interest. Like Judith, they too might have been applying the old workplace rules to this new workplace situation, which only served to reinforce her counterproductive reactions. They reacted to her anticipated promotion with advice such as: "Don't worry, you'll get the new job" or "If anyone around here deserves this promotion, you do." Such encouraging feedback added to Judith's anticipation of the promotion. Also, knowing that other people expected her to be promoted and had a stake in it added to the personal importance of the promotion.

When Judith's friends and family learned that she had been passed up for the promotion, they were shocked and disappointed for her. They took on her feelings as their own with such comments as: "I simply don't believe it, after all that you've done!" "Boy am I angry!" "You should sue." "If I were you, I wouldn't stay."

When her reaction began to take an obvious toll on her health, Judith's allies offered such suggestions as: "The president was always good to you, go to him." "Go over the director's head, you have nothing to lose."

Judith got a lot of feedback from people in her life who cared about her. They were on her side and personally angry for her. But their feedback only encouraged her to take it personally and to take actions based on her personal feelings. What Judith and her allies did not realize was that all of her impassioned determination would not reverse the company's carefully formulated plans. These plans were made based on what the decision makers had determined would be in the company's best interest. Judith's well-meaning allies reinforced and further encouraged her anger and indignation.

The support and encouragement of allies are certainly crucial. However, our allies often do and say things that go beyond their qualifications. They influence our perception of our situation, how we feel about the situation, and what actions we should take. This can lead us to take action that is based on the feedback of someone who has much less information and understanding than we do.

We must be clear about what our allies can and cannot do for us. For instance, if we encounter a serious medical or legal situation, we may turn to our allies for support and encouragement; but we do not expect them to give us legal or medical advice. Similarly, if we are trying to learn a new skill, we may turn to our allies for encouragement and support. They may also share our excitement and apprehension. However, when it comes to receiving the actual training, we will attend a school or training program. Qualified allies know their boundaries. They know when to defer to the experts. Unfortunately, when we are facing the uncertainty of the new workplace, this rule is often broken.

Judith needed to learn how to best utilize the people around her. She needed to know that these people could be either helpful or harmful. She needed to be clear about the boundaries of their role as allies. Unfortunately, Judith and her allies were not qualified to deal with the new workplace. She needed knowledgeable supporters. These knowledgeable supporters are her mentors, and we will discuss them next.

Mentors: Our Guides in the New Workplace

Just as companies undergoing change amass a pool of experts guiding their actions, so must you have your own experts to give you the right kinds of feedback and support. Even if Judith, for example, were able to self-manage and had effective allies, she would still be in a work world that was hard to understand and difficult to handle. She had never been in this type of workplace before and was not prepared to deal with it. For her, everything seemed so irrational. When she did take action, it often seemed to backfire. Furthermore, by the time she took one action, another unpredictable change was rumored or had occurred. Being in the middle of all these changes made it hard for her to see the whole picture. Judith needed someone who was knowledgeable. She needed someone who could help her understand what was happening and formulate the best plan and carry it out. She needed a mentor.

How could Judith have handled her situation differently? Let's imagine that she spoke with a cousin who was also acting in the spirit of ally. This ally would have shown concern, encouragement, and support. Ideally, she would have understood her limitations, and recommended that Judith find someone more qualified to serve as her mentor. Her cousin's husband might be just the right person. After all, he had been a manager in both the old and the new workplace. He had a business and had knowledge of how decisions are made and carried out. He was also a good listener, was very objective, knew when to state his views, and was available to Judith.

One of the first things Judith's qualified mentor might have done would have been to encourage her to look at the possible reasons someone else was appointed director. Her mentor probably would have had her look for the business rationale because most likely that is why the other person was chosen. The two of them would have figured out that the new director had power delegated by the president. It would have been clear that he was the person she had to relate to. Instead of declaring a war that she was destined to lose, her best bet would have been to try to win him over. This would have been in Judith's best interest. She would then have been able to make decisions based on understanding rather than personal reactions.

If Judith had had such an effective mentor, she probably would have begun to understand that the director was not implementing his personal policies but was a messenger of management doing what the company wanted. This is an entirely different picture from the one Judith painted without the help of her mentor. The new picture is that of a company that decided it needed to cut costs and as a result had to make greater demands on its employees. It hired someone who could and would make these changes. Could it be that Judith was seen as too loyal and too bound to the old policies to be trusted to effectively manage these changes?

An effective mentor also would have discouraged Judith's conversation with the president. He would have understood how her manager's self-interest was linked with the president's. Even if it had helped in the short-term, it would not have been an effective long-term strategy.

We have already discussed some of the basic rules of the new workplace:

- ☑ Don't take it personally.
- ☑ Look out for your self-interest.
- ☑ Broaden your vision.
- ☑ Don't be too loyal.
- ☑ Manage yourself.
- ☑ Increase your value to the workplace.
- ☑ Balance personal and work life.
- ☑ You can't succeed alone.

All of these things are a lot easier said than done. No matter how knowledgeable and experienced you are, when you are in the middle of it all, you can lose focus and objectivity. It can be tricky. You will need a mentor to guide you.

Selecting an Effective Mentor

If you choose a professional coach as one of your mentors, do your research. Ask for references from people you trust, your professional association, or a former teacher whom you trust. Do not confuse a counselor who helps you with your stress or emotional concerns with a mentor unless he or she also has proven expertise in workplace matters.

You also need to be able to "fire" a mentor. If it's not working out, you must move on. You cannot allow concerns about family tension, social discomfort, or professional embarrassment to lock you in.

The following checklist will help you in selecting an effective mentor.

assessment three

Effective Mentor Checklist

	True	False
1. My mentor understands the importance of not taking events and situations in the workplace personally; nor does my mentor react personally, impose his or her feelings on me, or judge me.	____	____
2. My mentor maintains the view of acting in my self-interest.	____	____
3. This person effectively communicates with me, is "on my wavelength," and commands my respect.	____	____
4. My mentor is knowledgeable about and has dealt effectively with challenging situations in the workplace.	____	____
5. This person is someone with whom I am comfortable and can be objective.	____	____
6. He or she is interested in learning about me, my situation, and my reactions.	____	____

	True	False

7. I am comfortable that this person is trustworthy; that is, I know he or she will not share my situation with other people without my permission and will be protective of my reputation.   ____   ____

8. I am comfortable approaching this person, and he or she is available to me.   ____   ____

9. My mentor listens to me and asks the right questions to help me understand what is happening.   ____   ____

10. My mentor helps me sort out among possibilities and find the action that makes the most sense and can be effectively carried out.   ____   ____

11. This person is flexible and able to adjust as needed.   ____   ____

If you answered "False" to any of these questions, you may want to discuss them with your mentor. If you answered "False" to many of the questions, it may be time to look for someone new.

Breaking the "Doing It Alone" Pattern

Even people who can see the benefits of having allies and mentors as a part of their support network can often think of a million reasons why they think they should not be seeking them out. Asking someone to be one's mentor can be especially hard the first time. Many people have difficulty asking others for advice or trusting someone with such an important matter when there is so much at stake. There are many reasons for this. Often they are too proud—in the old workplace, they were taught to be "independent." Perhaps they are simply too embarrassed. "Doing It Alone" becomes a pattern that is hard to break. Asking for help either does not come to their mind or, when it does, is rejected immediately. But in order to be successful in the new workplace, one must seek out and effectively utilize mentors.

Tony decided to tackle some of his work problems by getting advice from a mentor. Since he had always prided himself on his independence, this was a big step for him. Tony approached this task like any other learning process. He began by identifying a mentor as we suggested above. He started a conversation by presenting a "hypothetical" situation as if it were about someone else. This made him feel less vulnerable. It went something like this:

> You know Lee, from time to time I have been asked how to handle certain situations. I give my opinion or suggestions but I'm always curious about what suggestions others might give. What about you? Do you ever wonder the same thing? I respect your opinions, so I'd like to share one with you. It's one that I know a lot of people are dealing with.

Afterward, he tested the water for doing this again with something like this:

> It always helps me to get someone else's read on a situation. If it's all right with you, maybe I could run other situations past you in the future?

Once Tony had gained some comfort with this interaction, he was able to talk about some more of his dilemmas.

What we want to emphasize is that you need to initiate this process. It's okay if you do it slowly and cautiously. You could try a casual approach in a casual setting. It could be while playing golf, working out in the gym, or sitting in the steam room.

Stay "In Training"

The new workplace can be filled with constant surprises, assaults, and challenges that can overwhelm you. It requires as much careful attention and study as any other important pursuit that you have engaged in. You are constantly "in training," and must adopt an attitude in which you keep this in mind.

Chances are, you've had mentors before, maybe without even realizing it. You can probably recall times in the past when you turned to people for help—maybe in school or on your first job. Perhaps these people were teachers, tutors, supervisors, mentors, consultants, or co-workers. They helped you understand the work world and helped you adopt success-oriented attitudes. Your mentor will help you maintain your workplace value through it all.

All this time, as you are benefiting from your discussions with your mentor, your important allies are still helping you maintain the balance you so desperately need.

Chapter 11

Moving Toward Mutuality

Imagine a team practicing for the big game. Then when it comes, the players go out and just try to destroy each other. Unfortunately, we see this all the time as work teams attempt to deal with the new workplace. The new workplace is already difficult enough for you and your company without everyone destroying each other. We hope that when these pressures arise, there will be a mutual understanding that everyone's interest is in the same direction—being successful and getting the job done. Yet, too often, the opposite happens. This is the time when people seem to do things that lead to conflict and alienation rather than mutuality. Instead of cooperative teams, enemy camps often arise. Unless there is an active effort to reverse the destructive process, it only progresses. It's a wonder that the job gets done at all.

Tim's work deteriorated when his department started laying people off. His manager, Alison, was overworked and under a great deal of pressure to produce. She called Tim's attention to his "sloppy work" and required that he check in with her twice a day. This was taking up too much of her attention. She did not have time for this and began to resent it. How dare he do such a lousy job, she thought. He knows how much pressure I'm under. Alison knew Tim could do much better. Everybody was overworked, not just him. He had to do his part. She did not have time to baby-sit.

Alison finally let Tim have it. She let him know that his work was unsatisfactory and that he needed to put in more effort and improve. After all, he knew how pressured everyone else was. Why should he expect anyone to hold his hand? She explained that he had been retained because it was felt that he could handle the new demands, and now he was expected to live up to that expectation.

Alison walked away from the encounter telling herself that she had done what she needed to do. She had straightened Tim out and let him know what was expected. She was sure that now Tim's work would turn around. It was a clear message that he had to hear.

Unfortunately, Alison could not control how Tim received her message. Tim became angry. He could not believe that after all he had contributed, he was now being treated like this! He kept thinking, All she had to do was take the time to discuss things with me; she didn't have to blast me the way she did!

He was incensed. He could not shake his anger and indignation and had difficulty concentrating. Furthermore, why would he want to come through for her now, after the way she had treated him? He decided he would show her! He would do the work accurately but take his time, and he would not let on how he really felt. In the meantime, he would start looking for opportunities with another company. As far as he was concerned, there were plenty of competitors that might be interested in him.

Tim was angry and hurt. He was focused on the attack and was insulted. He felt that his manager had turned against him, and this moved him farther away from her. He could not see himself remaining on Alison's team—in fact, he could not imagine being on her side. He no longer had an obligation to Alison. He wanted revenge and could hardly wait to see her reaction when he broke the news that he was leaving. In Tim's mind, he would win and Alison would lose. In reality, Tim, who had worked hard to develop a positive track record and reputation in a strong company, had now chosen to go out and start over in another company.

Alison thought that laying down the law would motivate Tim to see the light. Nothing else she had done had worked. In her mind, she had sent a clear message and gotten his attention. He would now see things her way. His slacking off would end. She saw it as a win-win situation in which she would get the effort she wanted from Tim, and Tim would keep his job. In reality, Alison lost an employee who had the potential to be a strong asset.

As you can see, this interaction led to a losing situation for both Tim and Alison. Alison was losing a strong employee whom she had intended to motivate. Tim was leaving a company in which he had worked for years and had established a career track. The price of losing was high for each.

What happened? Both Tim and Alison were under a lot of pressure and only able to view things from their own pressured lens. There was no room to see where the other person was coming from. In fact, there was no desire to see it. Besides, there was so much anger, resentment, and mistrust that it was easier for them to take aim at each other. This only reduced each other's chance for success.

Neither knew what the other was thinking or feeling. Therefore, neither had the information needed to make it a true win-win situation. They could not work to patch it up, because each mistakenly thought that he or she saw the complete picture. How could they come to a mutually beneficial solution if each only saw half of the picture—theirs? The basic solution to this losing outcome is for them to recognize that if one loses, so does the other. They need to be aware that one person's success will likely elevate the other's. They need to work together and to benefit mutually.

Moving toward mutuality means first working to view things through the other person's eyes in order to achieve a win-win outcome. With Tim and Alison, it means going beyond their own pressures and acknowledging that the changes are also taking a toll on the other person. It may mean cutting the other person a little slack. Moving toward mutuality requires skill and work. In this chapter, we will show you how to start.

Recognizing the "Everyone Out for Himself or Herself" Attitude

These pressured times seem to promote an "Everyone Out for Himself or Herself" attitude. With Tim and Alison, this started about three years ago when a national competitor decided to go after a particular market. The competing company geared up by hiring a group of aggressive managers at relatively low wages. They were able to launch an aggressive marketing campaign and cut prices. Tim and Alison's company was the target. This was a major threat to its existence.

The board of directors, stockholders, and upper management had no choice but to respond to this threat by cutting costs and finding ways to operate more efficiently. Additional demands were put on senior managers. These changes were swift. Each manager had to come up with plans for cutting back in his or her department. The cost-cutting goals were very ambitious. This meant cutting the workforce at all levels, including managers. Alison had been given the unenviable task of delivering the layoff message to her people. It was while under this pressure that Alison was also dealing with Tim's lack of productivity.

If we charted the typical chain of events leading to the "Everyone Out for Himself or Herself" attitude, it would look something like this:

FIGURE 2

PRESSURE SPIRAL

Marketplace forces

Put pressures on the company in the form of increased competition, decrease of market share, mergers, acquisitions, other change in the world economy, or pressure from stockholders or investors.

↓

Upper management responds

Decides how to respond to the above forces and meet the demands of the stockholders represented by the board of directors. These could include reducing or freezing compensation, restructuring and redeploying workers, laying off or demoting senior managers.

↓

Senior management responds

Develops a plan for its divisions to comply with the cost-cutting demands placed on them. This could include restructuring the divisions and laying off or demoting managers.

↓

Directors respond

Develop a plan for their departments to meet these efficiency and cost-cutting demands. These might include deciding how to cut costs and deploy the workforce and determining who will be laid off.

↓

Managers respond

Comply with their managers' demands to cut costs by making recommendations for layoff candidates and determining other cost-cutting measures. They are also typically responsible for conveying layoff messages to employees. They need to make sure that their team complies with the new productivity demands.

↓

Employees respond

Do their jobs despite the new demands and structure.

As you can see, the pressure hits all of the workplace players. It is passed from the top to the bottom of the ladder. They are all in it together, and can either sink together or swim together.

Neutralizing the "My Manager Is Rotten" Attitude

We believe that Tim had a choice. He could focus his attention on what Alison had done to him—on how wrong and unfair she had been in doing this to him—or he could work to get beyond his view and see the big picture. This means understanding the chain of events leading to the "Everyone Out for Himself or Herself" attitude.

Perhaps then he could see things differently. We hope he would be able to see how Alison thought that what she was doing would get through to him. After all, she had seemed overwhelmed and desperate to get him to do the work. This might have been the only way she knew.

On the other hand, just because Alison did not deliver the message well, Tim was not justified in practicing bad self-management. The fact is that during these times of "doing more with less," many people are pressured and stressed. He needed to use some of the techniques we have discussed in this book to effectively manage himself and his workplace players.

It would have been to Tim's advantage to take control of the interaction. He needed to give Alison a message that indicated mutuality—that is, that viewed things through her eyes and suggested that she look through his. He first needed to acknowledge her view and reach out for where she was coming from with such remarks as: "I appreciate your feedback and want to know more about what you are seeing because I'll try to correct it." "I'm sorry that I'm adding to what must be a tremendous amount of pressure that you are carrying already." "You must be under a great deal of pressure."

He could then have offered his own experience and reaction to the pressure: "I'm sorry, I know that I haven't been performing up to par. The changes have been getting me down." Finally, he needed to leave her with what she needed—reassurance that he would get the job done: "I'll turn it around. Thanks for the message." More than likely, Alison would have responded in a way that said she understood his stress and that she would appreciate his renewed effort.

If Tim knew that the assignment deadline was out of his reach, it would have been to their mutual advantage to talk about this openly and find an achievable solution. He could have said that he would do his best but might need more time to complete everything. The next question is one of priorities. Tim and Alison needed to agree on what was most important, what needed to be done first, and what, if anything, could wait.

Such mutual interactions wouldn't mean anything if Tim didn't then "walk the walk." They required that he work hard to put his words into action. He had to show that he was doing what he could to carry out his part of the agreement so that Alison wouldn't have to worry about his work and his efforts. She needed to know that he would come through. He needed to know that if there were a problem, he could go to her to work toward a mutual solution.

Tim's move toward mutuality could be gradual. If he stayed focused he would succeed. If Alison were too heated to respond, he could leave the interaction and try again after the pressure subsided. It might take more than one time, but he would eventually gain if he moved toward mutuality with his manager.

It is important to try to see your manager's point of view. Don't forget that he or she is merely the messenger and is part of the reactionary chain that leads to the "Everyone Out for Himself or Herself" attitude. Remember to focus on the messenger and the message, not on how it is delivered. You can turn a bad message into a mutual venture. However, you can only control your part, not the outcome.

The following exercise will help you recognize whether you have elements of the "My Manager Is Rotten" attitude and move toward mutuality with your manager.

assessment four

Mutuality with Your Manager

	Yes	No
1. Do you focus on the messenger (manager) and the message instead of the delivery style?	____	____
2. Do you use self-management skills to keep from reacting personally?	____	____
3. Are you able to recognize that your manager has his or her pressures and as a result may convey nonmutual messages?	____	____
4. Do you consider your manager's viewpoint?	____	____
5. Do you focus on the outcome your manager hopes to achieve when a message is communicated?	____	____
6. Do you convey to your manager that you hear the message?	____	____
7. Do you convey to your manager that you will try to respond to the message?	____	____
8. Do you share your viewpoint with the goal of achieving understanding?	____	____
9. Do you work with your manager toward reaching a solution that serves the self-interest of each of you?	____	____
10. Are you prepared to pull back and try again if your manager does not respond with mutuality?	____	____
11. Do you put your full effort into doing the job?	____	____
12. Do you advise your manager of obstacles or your inability to fulfill certain requirements?	____	____
13. Do you recommend, mutually formulate, and work on possible solutions with your manager?	____	____
14. Do you follow up with your manager?	____	____

If you answered "No" to any of these questions, you may have elements of the "My Manager Is Rotten" attitude. If you would like to study a mutuality method that will increase these skills, you may want to refer to the book Getting to Yes *by Roger Fisher and William Ury.*

Avoiding the "Suffering in Silence" Attitude

We encounter many workers who selflessly do more than their share and get little in return. Their level of commitment is always above standard. They are the ones whom management can always count on. They accept and complete any assignment. They are totally loyal and never complain. They usually outshine their co-workers.

Yet, they never ask for anything in return. They do not ask for special recognition, increased compensation, or promotions. They often play themselves down. They appear to get gratification from doing a job well and being good team players. They may seem like the ideal employees. However, on closer examination, something is missing. Where's the mutuality? Let's take a look.

Simone was such an employee. She was an administrative assistant in an import company. Her office was always hectic and filled with demands. When her boss had an overload of work, Simone was called upon to do follow-up calls and complete reports for him. When salespeople were in a jam, she was called upon to do the backup work for them involving customers, suppliers, and shippers. It was always assumed that whatever was put on her desk would be done correctly—and, amazingly, it always was.

Simone always felt that she had to do the best that she could despite the pressures and effort that she had to put in. If she was asked to do something, she could not say no. The thought of not completing an assignment was entirely unacceptable; she put in whatever effort was necessary to get it done. This often left her stressed out and tired.

Simone often felt that what was happening was unfair. She wondered why she seemed to be working harder than most of her co-workers. When better career opportunities arose, she asked herself why she was not approached or at least given a choice. It would be a way of acknowledging all that she did. She also knew that she was working much harder than people who made much more money. Everybody there knew that she could not say no and that she would not ask for anything in return.

After her company downsized, several administrative and sales positions were eliminated. Because of her fine work, Simone was retained. Suddenly the same amount of work had to be done by a smaller workforce. Now her manager and the remaining sales-people were under even more pressure. They began to give her a lot more of their work to do, with little regard for the impact this was having on her. The work was too much for anyone, yet she still could not say no. As far as she was concerned, saying no would be a sign of failure.

As the stress built to unbearable levels, things that she had once viewed only as unfair now began to build up to resentments and even anger. This anger increased even more as she had to contend with difficulty sleeping, stomach problems, and overall fatigue. It got to the point that she could not even bear getting up in the morning.

One day, Simone decided she had had enough. She walked into her manager's office and told him she wanted to resign. Shocked, her manager tried to discuss things with her. Simone was so angry that she could not even listen to what he had to say. She couldn't leave his office fast enough.

Like many silent sufferers, Simone just suddenly reached her boiling point. Under the pressure of a changing workplace, her personal anger flooded into her professional role and she took a drastic measure to relieve her personal stress.

For some silent sufferers, medical and stress-related problems result in the need for extended absences and difficulty in keeping up the pace at work. For others, the resentments and anger become so overwhelming that they try to get co-workers to take their side. Too often they compromise their professionalism by saying unflattering things about management or co-workers. Some openly express their resentments by being disruptive. Silently suffering can lead to counterproductive actions that could sabotage a potentially promising career. Formerly trusting and respecting allies become embittered adversaries.

Quitting would result in a loss for both Simone and the company. She would compromise her chance to build a career in a company in which she had a strong track record. She would also burn bridges with no job to go to and no references. Her manager was in a high-stress environment with an administrative crisis. His salespeople would lose a major resource. Their ability to conduct business faced a major setback.

Silent sufferers, in part, create their own problems. By playing the role of the silent sufferer, Simone sent out the message that all was fine. The company was getting what it needed from her and more, and she did not let them know she was unhappy. As we have seen, management can be caught up with their own pressures, particularly with the arrival of the new workplace. They often respond only to those requests that are effectively presented or those that are persistently presented. Silent sufferers do not make such presentations.

The first thing Simone needed to do was give up the "Suffering in Silence" attitude. She needed to acknowledge to herself that she deserved better—perhaps advancement or more money. Second, she needed to be willing to take a big risk. After all, until now she had succeeded because at least she got praised. Was she willing to risk this in order to request a salary increase that she might not get or request a position in which there was uncertainty and possible failure?

Next, Simone needed to ask herself what it was that she specifically wanted. She might not want anything more than relief and a reduction of her workload. If so, was she willing to risk letting others know that she was unable to handle it? What would she do if they denied her request? What if they reduced her responsibility and her sense of importance also decreased? These are questions that she had to address before taking action. Her answers would guide her.

Simone also needed to learn how to communicate her request to management. Perhaps she had done this with less important matters and could draw on those experiences in learning how to assert herself. She would probably need to be assertive just to get the time she needed to talk with her manager in a hectic work environment. However, she needed to use her own initiative to make sure that this meeting took place. A simple statement with no compromise would do the trick. Here's an example: "I need some time to talk with you. It has to do with my future with our company"; or "I'm concerned, and need to talk with you about my position. I think that this will require our undivided attention. When shall we meet?"

Next would come the actual meeting. If she were looking for advancement, she could start with a question, for instance: "I have worked here for seven years, I like working for you and would like to see this company in my future. However, I wonder how you see it. What do you see as my career path?" This would be a declaration that she wanted her career to be considered.

Any response would give Simone a great deal of useful information. After she heard her manager out, she could share some of her ideas. This discussion would be a negotiation of sorts and could include such questions as the following: "What are your thoughts about my work and my qualifications?" "What are the possibilities of other positions opening up?" "What do I need to do to get the opportunity?" "What are your thoughts about my work and qualifications?" Ideally, it would be good if they left the meeting with a commitment that they would both think about what had happened and talk again. It would be important for Simone to set up a follow-up meeting to see how things were progressing.

If she wanted a pay raise, Simone could start off by indicating her appreciation for being trusted and having her skills recognized and valued as evidenced by being given the additional responsibility. She could also add her commitment to continuing doing quality work. She could then add that she was concerned that her compensation did not reflect her increased responsibility and workload. If needed, she should be ready to give examples.

Similarly, if she wanted a reduction in her workload, in addition to tooting her own horn about her skills and handling the heavy workload, she could also indicate that the assignment was more than any one person could effectively handle. She needed to be ready to back this up with concrete examples. She could then indicate that despite her best efforts, she might have to neglect some other important matters. Of course, she should voice her concern about the consequences of not doing the other work. She might even suggest a possible solution path, such as adding a part-time person with less skill and at a lower cost to do some of her more routine tasks. She could even offer to take on the responsibility of training and overseeing that person.

Simone's major goal is to create a win-win situation. She needs to work toward seeing herself winning. However, management also has to come away seeing this as a win for them. Whether it's a promotion, a raise, or a change in workload, an approach involving mutuality is always best.

Regardless of what happens, Simone cannot lose. After all, even if she does not get what she wants, she still will have gotten information that will help her make her decision about whether to stay or leave the company. Such information will also help her make a more graceful exit on her own terms in her own time.

Are you a silent sufferer? It may be to your and your company's advantage to move toward mutuality. Start by answering some key questions in Exercise 10.

exercise 10

Moving from Silent Suffering to Mutuality

1. Make a list of what you want changed. Then rate these items in importance on a scale of 1 to 10 (1 being most important). Now rate them again on the basis of how important you feel they are to the company.

	Importance to You	*Importance to Company*
Things to Change		
_____	____	____
_____	____	____
_____	____	____
_____	____	____

2. Anticipate how the company is likely to view your proposal; think of how other similar situations in the company were handled. List them below.

3. Explore several win-win scenarios. How can you and the company get what you want?

4. Decide how you will present your case to your manager. What communications approach is best with him or her?

5. How is your manager likely to respond to your proposal?

6. What negotiation strategy could be beneficial in working toward a mutual solution?

A mutual solution is the only one that will be effective. That means that you have to be ready to hear where your manager is coming from. You may want to prepare for this by just thinking about his or her point of view and the current situation the company is in. Books that we have mentioned such as *Your Perfect Right,* by Robert Alberti and Michael Emmons, and *Getting to Yes,* by Roger Fisher and William Ury, might help her prepare for this process.

Remember that action counts. Take action agreed to at your meeting. If not, play poker and plan to leave. Remember also that you are changing the rules. Your manager, who is used to seeing you conduct yourself in a certain way, may react to this major change with surprise or reluctance. Therefore, you cannot go into your meeting with the mind-set that you have lost if you fail to get everything you want. You will need to be a little flexible and to have several acceptable solutions in mind. Eventually, both you and your manager will have to go away feeling that you have won.

Enhancing Your Employees' Performance

Up to now we've looked at the situation from the employees' viewpoint. If it is to be truly mutual, we also have to look at how you see it if you are a manager. As a manager, you are upper management's messenger. You must remember that you interact with your employees with a basic understanding: They come to work and get paid; in return for this, they are expected to do their job. Your job is to represent the payer (the company) and make sure the job gets done.

Effective management, however, goes well beyond the basic agreement. Things are much more complex than simply paying and being paid. In fact, you and most of your employees will be working for many things less tangible than a paycheck.

Let's revisit Tim and Alison and get further into their story. As long as Tim was getting clear direction and positive, encouraging feedback, he felt good about devoting his full energy to performing his job. But once Alison, under pressure, began to micromanage his work, he spent most of his time just feeling stifled and angry. He was being squelched and felt defeated. These feelings replaced the enjoyment he had once associated with his job. It also took his focus and energy off of the actual job assignment. Alison was clearly doing things that distracted Tim from being productive.

Alison was violating the basic agreement. Tim was there to do his job effectively. Alison's job was to help him be as effective as he could be. Unfortunately, that didn't happen. She was getting in his way.

From our experience, most employees want to keep up their end of the bargain. Of course, they vary in degree of productivity and creativity, but even then, most say they want to do a great job. They want to try approaches to enhance their effort and their work. For the most part, they recognize that ideally there should be mutual interests for them and the company. The manager is effectively carrying out his or her side of the agreement if what he or she does encourages this type of behavior from an employee. The manager is also upper management's messenger in encouraging the best possible performance from his or her employees. A manager's self-interest is best served by being a job performance enhancer. This has mutual impact all the way up the chain.

As a manager, you have the best chance of enhancing job performance by focusing on mutuality. Your focus has to be on how your employees view things. If you are to motivate your employees to do their best, you will need to know what motivates them. To do this, you need to know how they perceive things and how they will receive your message. To do or say something that will discourage an employee's performance is acting contrary to your self-interest and that of your company.

Alison's job was to make sure that assignments were clear and that she gave Tim balanced feedback about his work. Tim believed that he was competent and that his work was important. This motivated him and propelled him forward.

When Alison felt that Tim's work was falling below standard, she had several options. She took the easy way, which was to reject and revise each of his efforts. The alternative, though more complicated in the short run, would be more effective because it involved helping Tim do what was needed to help her deliver what the company needed.

As a manager working toward mutuality, Alison's attention had to be on Tim as a contributor. She needed to study his work and look for his strengths and build on them. She also needed to determine the particular areas Tim needed to change and then consider what communications approach was likely to be most effective in conveying this message to him. She wanted him to be receptive, not defensive, so she needed to present her concerns accordingly and keep following up with him later. In this way, Tim could add value to her team and to the company.

Different people have different motivators. In our previous example, encouragement, realistic feedback, and presenting methods for change were the major motivators for Tim. Knowing that they are being monitored and that there are consequences for not doing their best motivates some people. Some are motivated by financial rewards for a job well done. Others are motivated by the satisfaction of doing a good job or by growing and learning. If you are a manager, take a few minutes right now and think about each of your employees' motivators.

Simone did not appear to need a motivator. She did her job and asked for nothing in return. Her manager did not take the time to learn more about her motivators. If he had, he would have saved himself a lot of trouble. He should have been able to see a strong performer not being rewarded for good performance—a total lack of mutuality. He needed to find out what was going on with her. As a representative of management, he should have attempted to recognize her efforts and to let her know that if she went out of her way to deliver for the company, the company would go out of its way to learn her point of view.

As a manager, you are critical to maintaining the quality and efficiency of your company. To do this, you need to appreciate and increase the value of your team and its members. The following exercise will help you.

exercise 11

Rating Yourself as Performance Enhancer

On a scale of 1 (totally incompetent) to 10 (excellent), rate your performance as manager in the following areas.

How good are you at:

Analyzing your employees' strengths?   _____

Analyzing their deficits?   _____

Determining what needs to change?   _____

Coaching and teaching your employees how to change?   _____

Knowing what motivates each employee?   _____

Viewing things through the eyes of individual employees?   _____

Being aware of your employees' general satisfaction levels?   _____

Rewarding them for their contributions?   _____

Try to work on those areas in which your rating is 5 or below. Remember, enhancing your employees' performance is in your own self-interest.

As a manager, you have probably been in the position of deciding whether an employee's efforts actually add value to the company. If so, you know how difficult it is, but you probably also know that working toward a mutual solution is crucial. Your first job is to work toward finding a way in which the employee can add value either by making suggestions on steps to improve performance or by changing the employee's assignment. If this is unsuccessful, there is no mutuality. That is when you have to let the employee know that his or her future with the company is in jeopardy.

Facilitating Between the Company and Employees

A manager must make sure that the team is performing most effectively as a unit. This requires a study of how the team is functioning. He or she needs to analyze and identify those things that enhance and those that diminish optimal team functioning. Is there a silent sufferer or another unhappy person spreading negative messages? Is a frustrated team member threatening the morale of the team? All of this will affect the performance of the team.

Remember Benesha from Chapter 1, who had the "I No Longer Have Any Friends" attitude? After she was promoted, she had to put pressure on her team to perform. She did so by delivering the message of "mutuality of misery." She also held them accountable. Unfortunately, she didn't think about how her team would view this message. She also gave little thought to what would motivate them. As a result, her approach led to a very negative reaction and a lot of negative energy. It was "them against her"—no mutuality.

If Benesha had tried to view things through their lens she might have presented the new demands differently. Instead of just sending the misery message, she also could have conveyed a message of mutuality. She could have asked for feedback and elicited their ideas about how to meet these demands. It could have been an opportunity to come together. She also could have offered to help them by first finding out what they perceived they needed.

The door would have been open to have a cooperative effort—she helps them and they help her.

Mutuality applies on all levels of the work organization. The manager needs his or her managers to do their job in order for his or her interest to be served. The same is true on up and down the ladder. The following chart illustrates the mutuality that a manager is trying to achieve as the facilitator between the company and the employees.

chart three

Responsibilities of Company, Manager, and Employee

Company	Manager	Employee
Produce product or service	Monitor and enforce performance	Do the work
Provide a paycheck	Recommend compensation	Receive pay
Provide superior product or service	Motivate, instruct	Take initiative, be creative
Compete/remain in business	Monitor, enforce	Work up to standard
Provide incentives	Recommend recipients	Offer superior performance
Provide leadership	Motivate, instruct	Work accurately and efficiently
Address unsatisfactory performance	Monitor, evaluate performance; enforce/ convey message	Put in extra effort; seek other opportunities

Always remember the need to maintain mutuality. With this in mind, whatever you can do to strategically increase your workplace value will add to your side of the mutuality scale. We suggest that you refer back to Chapter 8, to refresh yourself on ways to increase your workplace value. As a manager, whatever you do to help your team member achieve this will be a win for you.

Chapter 12

Shining Your Own Light

We often see very successful people suddenly question their competence when the new workplace hits them. They believe that a decision made by their new management suddenly tells them the whole truth about their worth. They begin to let the external messages take over their internal messages.

One of the first steps on the journey to success is to be able to see your own light. What most successful people have over others is that they do not allow any circumstances to fully control their attitude toward themselves. They maintain a determination to recognize their strengths and acknowledge their competence. They know that negative events can affect their self-confidence, but they work hard to maintain a belief in themselves. What pushes them forward is the knowledge that they have what it takes, and at times they have to use their inner searchlight to keep it glowing. That knowledge and determination fuel them. They exude confidence. The more difficult the situation, the more determined they are to prove to themselves that they can do it. It is just as important for them to prove this to themselves as it is for them to demonstrate it to others.

Don't Let Your Light Dim

Throughout this book, we have shown how quickly a competent worker can come to believe that he or she is incompetent. These were successful people who did their work very well and were positively regarded by their employers. Then things changed. They were either laid off or denied their promised promotions. Suddenly they began to doubt themselves and question their ability. Their thinking was that if they were good they would be "wanted" or rewarded with a promotion. They were sure that they did not measure up and began to wonder whether they ever had.

In this new workplace, many workers get less feedback—positive or negative—from their increasingly burdened managers. If they are given any feedback, it is usually when unsatisfactory work performance has to be corrected. When this happens, they often begin to question their competence. After all, many workers look to their managers to tell them about the value of their work. It's the way it used to be.

Many of our friends were able to work enthusiastically and to feel good about themselves and their abilities only as long as they were getting positive feedback from their manager. When the changes occurring in the workplace resulted in different expectations, they began receiving negative feedback. They echoed this feedback to themselves. They even questioned whether they were ever talented.

Often when the changes come, managers feel overwhelmed. The smiles, words of encouragement, and positive feedback employees are used to may suddenly stop. Employees may assume that the manager is questioning their work and their competence, even though the quality of their work has not changed. The question becomes whether the previous positive feedback was ever sincere or whether no feedback now means they are not performing well.

We know that none of our aforementioned friends all of a sudden became incompetent when the new workplace arrived. They did not lose their talent the day that their company merged with another or lose their ability to manage after having done it successfully for many years. Our friends didn't change, the world around them changed. With this changing world, they changed their view of their accomplishments. The lack of feedback had dimmed their light, causing them to view their past through the same dim light. They forgot their past successes. Their past accomplishments were no longer real. Their previous successes were even doubted.

If the dim light of the new workplace is distorting your memory of your competence and achievements, we recommend that you change it. Set the record straight. Don't lie to yourself. Rather, remember your real achievements, successes, competencies, and positive feedback from the past. Credit yourself. Restore the bright lights of your career. Use the following exercise to help you recall and restore your history. In other words, we want you to reminisce—do a little daydreaming. We hope this will help you find that light and set the record straight.

exercise 12

Restoring Your Memory Banks

1. Recall your past achievements and successes. (Looking over your résumé may help). List them below.

2. Look over your list in item #1. Consider the skills you used to achieve those successes and list them below.

3. What are your passions? (Chances are, therein lie some of your talents as well.)

4. What do you think you are good at?

5. What have others told you that you were good at? Who were those people? In what setting was this feedback given? (Can you call on allies to help you remember?)

Whatever competence you had you still have. Whatever positive feedback you received was probably because of your ability. Whatever skills you needed to succeed you still have. Your knowledge is still yours, despite the realities of the new workplace. You still bring all of your assets with you. They are yours and are waiting to be used. But you need to build on them and learn to use them in a different way.

Make sure your light is not dimmed by someone else. It's up to you. You have a choice. For instance, if you have a negative manager, you can choose not to reflect his or her style. This negativity is the manager's; it is not about you. Managers can have a tremendous impact on you, but you will need to shine your light regardless of your manager's style. The following are some rules to follow.

chart four

Rules for Shining Your Light

- Go for your own inner fuel and use it to shine your light.
- Use your inner light to shine outward.
- Remind yourself of your ability.
- Look back at your achievements and endurance record.
- Talk with people who will remind you of your competence.
- Use that energy to fuel you.

You can do yourself the favor of shining a light that comes from within you. Don't forget, you are doing this for yourself, not for your manager or anyone else. It is this light that you need to propel you forward, professionally and personally. If you have discouraging events or memories, stop yourself and remember your competencies and successes. They're still yours. They fuel your inner light that will shine outward.

Try Walking in Your Manager's Shoes

Let's play a game. It's called "Walking in Your Manager's Shoes." Imagine your company is undergoing a major downsizing and it is up to you to choose who goes and who stays. Let's say that out of five employees who have the same skills and seniority, one is to be promoted. What choice would you make? Would that person be you?

Here are their descriptions:

☑ *Employee A* is quiet and reserved and generally does what he is told. He is never enthusiastic but is very focused on his work.

☑ *Employee B* is often negative and unhappy. He usually doesn't like getting new assignments and complains if there is too much work.

☑ *Employee C* is generally enthusiastic and comes to work with a smile. She tackles the work that is given to her and does not hesitate to take on special assignments.

☑ *Employee D* works very hard and often makes it a point to ask if there are any opportunities. When others are promoted, he usually voices his disappointment and is not shy about letting people know how unfair he thinks it is.

☑ *Employee E* works hard and is generally positive even though you hear through the grapevine that she often complains about you behind your back.

Now in putting yourself in your manager's shoes, you may realize that you are discouraged yourself. Some of your workers pick up on your discouragement and begin to convey their own discouragement. Who would you likely gravitate toward to keep—the negative team members or the others? We hope you would move toward those with a light shining. We hope you would not be moving toward someone who is looking to be uplifted, reassured, and constantly stroked. Actually, such a worker may not know how, or even want, to be uplifted. This person does not have a sustaining inner light and may be in the habit of seeing the negative and asking for payback for everything that he or she does. Not only would this person be an extra burden on you, his or her attitude might even rub off on your team.

We hope you chose Employee C—Diana. As a manager, you know that she will do the work and can be counted on to take on what has to be done. You would not have to worry about complaints, a negative attitude, or special requests and demands. Your job is hard enough as it is—you do not need to be around someone who brings you down emotionally. Why not benefit from the positive energy and initiative of your employees? That is the requirement for success, especially in the new workplace. Now let's hear the stories of two of the aforementioned anonymous employees.

Garret (Employee D) worked in an investment house. He was very ambitious and was anxious for advancement. He had a co-worker, Diana, who was very competitive. Diana was constantly volunteering to take on special assignments and did them in addition to her own work. No matter how tough things were, Diana would come in vibrant and ready to do another day's work. Garret became devastated. He only wanted a few minutes with his manager to talk about opportunities that he felt he deserved. He never got them. He came to work overwhelmed and clearly concerned about his lack of recognition. His description of Diana was of a "phony" who would do anything to cozy up to the boss. He was obviously demoralized. When a promotion came up, Diana got it. It wasn't even a contest. Garret became even more disheartened. Now that Diana was gone, his hope was that he would be next in line.

Why did Diana get chosen for the promotion? If you were the manager, who would you choose? Who would you select to get the job done? Who would you look forward to seeing at the work site? Who would you want to keep on your team in the event of a layoff? Who would you look to promote and give more responsibility?

In the new workplace, in order to get ahead and be successful, Garret will need to shine his light. Here are some things he can start with:

☑ Doing work assignments with enthusiasm and energy
☑ Maintaining a positive attitude and avoiding complaining
☑ Offering solutions to his manager's constructive criticism
☑ Being committed to sharing the work burden
☑ Being ready to take on extra assignments

However, even then, he may not get, nor should he expect, an immediate payoff. Nonetheless, his light must remain shining. All things being equal, Garret's day will come. Maybe his opportunities will come in the form of surviving another layoff, getting growth-oriented assignments, having interesting opportunities in other parts of the company, and being promoted. All of these outcomes are better than the alternatives. They are the payoffs for shining your own light.

Of course, if he does not get the opportunities he feels he deserves or that he is looking for, he could focus his searchlight elsewhere. Even then, he should remember the importance of not taking it personally. He very well may be in another situation where his light is bright but his department doesn't have the right opportunities or a co-worker has more suitable qualifications or a brighter or more focused light. This is no time to get discouraged. Now is the time to shine the light more brightly and broadly.

If you find yourself in this type of situation, you need to take the pulse of your company. Stay in touch with your co-workers and try to be more visible than before. Make sure that your positive attitude, energy, commitment, and knowledge shine through. If something comes up in another department, you may be the person to fill the job. It is important to be visible and be seen in a good light at all times, not just when you are seeking and interviewing for a job. The fact is, you are always being considered for other positions, whether you know it or not. People are watching.

As a manager, whom would you want to work with? The successful people we know would choose someone who shines his or her light. Keep this in mind as you interact with your colleagues. Make sure you shine yours.

Carry Your Light with You

Wherever you go, let your light shine. Your job is not just "at work"; it extends to meetings, training sessions and other types of classes, and involvement with organizations that include your colleagues or potential colleagues. These all present opportunities for you to shine your light.

As we discussed in Chapter 8, professions have all kinds of associations and organizations that rely on volunteers to survive. Every committee and task force requires the involvement of members in order to be successful. There are many ways to be seen as effective and ways to make contributions. Involvement in professional, fraternal, or alumni associations or in unions can give you a lot of visibility. You have many choices. Identifying your personal style will help you narrow down specific ways you can contribute to these organizations and associations. The following assessment will help.

assessment five
....

Identifying Your Personal Style

Put a check mark next to each of the statements in the following categories that applies to you. Note the categories into which you fall—there may be more than one. Then read the style descriptions that follow.

Category A

I like to get involved in the nitty-gritty work.	_____
I willingly take on the work.	_____
I get things done.	_____
I like to take on a task and see it through to the end.	_____
I am more comfortable interacting socially if it is around a task.	_____

Category B

I have the ability to head up projects.	_____
I am good at leading meetings.	_____
I am good at encouraging people to work together.	_____
I can motivate others.	_____
I like being visible.	_____

Category C

I generally get along well with others.   _____

I am comfortable with a lot of interaction.   _____

I have the ability to put people at ease.   _____

I am good at listening.   _____

I have good communication skills.   _____

Category D

I like organization-level politics.   _____

I am a good decision maker.   _____

I am a good consensus builder.   _____

STYLE DESCRIPTIONS

A. Task-oriented style

With a task-oriented style, you can shine your light by putting on a seminar or conference, working on a project, or helping carry out the day-to-day functioning. Make sure your light is positive, energetic, collaborative, and goal oriented.

B. Leadership style

Every group needs the light of leadership. Every organization has its leadership, every committee has a chairperson, and every project has a director. Shine your leadership light.

C. People-focused style

Every professional organization needs to have members who relate to the membership and encourage them to get involved. They can serve on membership committees and as elected leaders.

D. Political style

Most professional associations and unions have national and local governing bodies. Each has a board of directors, both in the central and local chapters. Alumni associations and other similar groups also have governing bodies. They are also in need of political types who will take on the tasks of governing.

Recognizing your personal style will help you to get involved in activities that you believe in and are worth your while—that is, those in which you can really invest positive energy and that excite you. Otherwise, you're defeating the purpose. People will learn about you based on your attitude and how you perform. Awareness of your personal style will help put you in the best light. Whether it's a professional, alumni, or fraternal association or union, your involvement will give you a professional home base beyond where you work. It's important to have such a professional base, especially if you change positions or employers, because you can continue growing with the same group of people.

There are many opportunities for you to shine your light. You just have to be ready and willing to get involved. Places of worship and civic and community organizations are often in search of members who are willing to take an active role in various activities. This might include becoming involved in a local political organization, school board or PTO, women's or men's club, or neighborhood association. Of course, the farther you are from your field, the less likely you are to be visible to fellow professionals. However, in addition to a general exposure, you may get the needed balance that we discussed in Chapter 9. Here you can be the expert accountant, lawyer, engineer, secretary, writer, artist, leader, or organizer. A wide audience awaits you. It includes anyone who is involved in or exposed to your professional organizations, your community agencies, and your other social activities.

As long as you keep your light shining inside, you will be able to shine it outward. In doing this you are marketing a most important product—yourself.

Pulling It All Together

All of the people you've met in this book can succeed in this new workplace if they remember that it isn't personal, act in their self-interest, and have the knowledge and skills we have identified. Let's imagine a scene in which some new workplace characters are working together and are having a discussion about what they've learned in the new workplace. They are determined to be successful and to help a co-worker who is struggling to leave the old workplace behind and enter into the new. Armed with the knowledge and skills contained in this book, they can help him learn and utilize the secrets of success.

Dramatic Scene from Imaginary Play

Success in the New Workplace

Dramatis Personae

Puzzled Oldworlder, who needs to understand what is happening to him and what he can do about it.

Alli Lovingworlder, who is on Puzzled's side and gives him acceptance, support, and sustenance, even though she knows less about what is happening than he does.

Sharply Changingworlder, a mentor who has figured out the rules of the new workplace.

Successful Neworlder, a mentor who not only has figured it out but has learned the secrets of success.

SCENE 1

Enter Puzzled Oldworlder

I spent eighteen years in this company. I worked hard, did all that was asked of me. I even developed friendships with my colleagues. I was as loyal as could be through the good and the bad times. Frankly, I'm a bit of a perfectionist and they at times joked about it, but they knew that if they wanted a job done right, I was the one to do it. I can't complain, though. It was a good old world. I was treated fairly and at times generously for my efforts. I was clearly on a strong career path and was told as much by management. They took a personal interest in me and I knew it. One thing was certain, success was pretty well guaranteed as long as I continued to do my part. I could see myself getting the thirty-year gold retirement watch.

Then came the bomb. At least it felt that way. We were successful and I guess that made us a target for a takeover. Before I knew it, another company acquired us. Suddenly my world fell apart. I was answering to a management that had very different ways of doing things. The first thing they did was look for ways to make us efficient. They called it downsizing, but it felt like murder. Watching my co-workers and friends get laid off was really tough. I survived. Talk about guilt! I can still see my laid-off co-workers. To add insult to injury, my former friends in management were the ones handing out the layoff notices. We had a personal commitment to each other, and they were breaking it. I couldn't believe it!

Everybody kept saying I was lucky. And you think survival meant that I was the lucky one? Well, of course, there was twice as much work, with half the people to do it. I found myself doing my work and that of my poor former co-workers, too. As if that wasn't tough enough, my perfectionism kicked in as I struggled to do it all, perfectly. I never had more tension and body aches in my life. The only time I had to myself was for a quick sandwich and a short night's sleep.

As if that wasn't bad enough, a position opened up—a position that I had been promised and groomed for. I was sure that it would be mine. Well, they hired an outsider for the position. I was beside myself with hurt and rage. What I had worked for all these years was now denied me. Why in the world did I believe them in the first place? Why did I do all that work and maintain all that loyalty? Things seemed to go downhill from there. The new manager was all demands and could rarely be pleased. This was one of the toughest parts. I could never do things well enough for him. Believe it or not, I began to question my own competence—after working there for eighteen years!

Now I'm at the end of my rope. I just can't take it any more. My family tells me I'm bringing my work pressures home and treating them badly. They tell me not to take it any more and to give them a piece of my mind. They just don't understand. I can't win anywhere. How do I deal with the tension, anger, and pain?

Enter Alli Lovingworlder

You haven't been yourself lately and I am really worried about you. You were never the most open person in the world, but at least you used to spend time with me and acted as if you cared about how I was doing. You also talked some about work and seemed to enjoy discussing it. I could always count on your support, and you seemed to value our friendship.

Since the changes at work, you're like a different person. Now when I see you, all you do is complain about work or sit around saying nothing with a worried look on your face. It hurts to see you like this. In fact, I am beginning to look forward to the times when you stay at work late and I don't see you at all.

When I heard how you were being treated at work, I expressed my anger and challenged you to fight back. Now I realize that it was not the most helpful approach I could have taken. In fact, I learned that I don't have the knowledge or the emotional distance to correctly advise you. You will need to talk to informed people about what you should do. I want to give you support. I also need to get the support and encouragement I need to get through this.

Enter Sharply Changingworlder

I really know what you are talking about. I had similar thoughts and went through very similar feelings. In fact, hearing you talk makes me feel a little less crazy. The main thing I needed to understand was that it just wasn't personal. I had always felt a personal commitment to the company and was shown that they had a personal commitment to me. That's over. Whether their personal commitment was real or not, it felt that way. Today it's all business. The only thing I can do is look out for my own self-interest. I constantly remind myself of this and ask myself the key question: What do I have to do to take care of my own self-interest?

I now know that past promises mean nothing. I look at the people who made these promises and now know that their power is not much greater than mine. Things are unpredictable for all of us. Things can change at a moment's notice for a lot of reasons. Some may appear to make sense and some won't. The company could have a new boss or a new owner tomorrow. A competitor could come in and change all the rules. So I see these supervisors and managers for what they are—messengers. They just pass on the latest rules and directions handed to them by the current upper management. I remain loyal, but only as it serves my self-interest.

I must confess I am a pessimist at heart. I'll tell you, at first this was my nightmare come true. I was constantly in a state of panic, waiting for the doom to fall. I guess that's why I had to work so hard to try to understand what was happening. That's why it was so difficult to get some control over myself. Frankly, I still have periods of fear and sudden panic. Now, what I do is use stress management exercises and techniques to calm myself. I'm getting there, but I haven't put it all together. Yet, I'm surviving and feel a lot better. I'm making a lot of progress, but I still don't know exactly how to achieve true success in the new workplace.

Enter Successful Neworlder

I truly know where the two of you are coming from. I've been there. I fully agree with what you are saying. However, I did learn how to take it a step further. I now take it for granted that I must have balance in my life. I know that I am one whole person and that each aspect of my life affects other aspects. I really have to work at managing myself in order for anything to work out. So I spend time with people I am emotionally close to. I exercise regularly and find ways to relax. I'm not completely thrown off guard when I'm stressed because I now expect to be stressed. The difference is that I have a regime of relaxers that help me manage my reactions when the heat is on.

I have also come to recognize that it truly is a new workplace. Things are changing quickly and unpredictably in my company and in the field. I will always have to be a learner. I will have to stay up on the latest in my company, my industry, and my field. I spend a good deal of time reading and attending various seminars. To keep up, I have also become more active in my professional association. Luckily, I have always been the energetic type. I do anything I can to be visible, to make sure that my skills are observed and valued by my managers and co-workers. If I haven't learned anything else I've learned the following: I know that success comes to those who are perceived as having value, who keep maintaining their value, who try, who are available, and who always come through. Success also means not being shy. Although I don't go around asking for things, I make it clear that I am interested in advancement and opportunities. I also have a guiding light that reaches for mutuality. We are all in the same boat. My sense is that the best thing I can do for myself is understand the pressures and demands that my managers and co-workers face and do my best to be an asset to them. I have nothing to lose in doing this. If they don't value and reward me for my effort, I can always look for other opportunities. I also have to confess that my loyalty to my company doesn't cause me to compromise my loyalty to myself. That's why I am aware of and open to other opportunities.

You may wonder where I get all of this energy. I have news for you, Puzzled. I probably utilize a lot less energy than you do. I am active and do what I need to do. I know what it's like to have all of the fear, negative thinking, and tension to contend with. Actually, being active and satisfied is a lot less tiring.

I also know that things are changing quickly all around me. Therefore, I won't always understand what is happening. There will be times when I will probably miss important things and not think of all of my best options. I'm not perfect. There may still be times when I get caught up in myself and let my emotions get in the way. To keep myself on track, I turn to certain people who know what's happening and are available to help me. I call them my mentors.

Exit all characters except Puzzled, looking thoughtful as lights fade

END PLAY

Alli Lovingworlder was able to learn about what in the workplace is so deeply affecting the life of her loved one. Sharply Changingworlder was able to get a better sense of what the new workplace is about, appreciate how far she has come, and learn how to achieve success. Successful Neworlder was able to expand his knowledge of the workplace, one of the secrets of his success. We are pleased to have included the knowledge and skills that helped Sharply Changingworlder, Alli Lovingworlder, and Successful Neworlder, and that will help Puzzled Oldworlders everywhere achieve success in the new workplace. The quest for success is an ongoing process and requires working together. We all have something to offer and something to gain. We suggest that you use this book as an ongoing guide, and we wish you the best.

References

Alberti, Robert, and Michael Emmons. *Your Perfect Right,* San Luis Obispo, CA: Impact Publishers, 1995.

Benson, Herbert. *The Relaxation Response,* New York: Morrow Books, 1975.

Burns, David. *Feeling Good: The New Mood Therapy.* New York: Avon Books, 1980.

Fast, Julius. *Body Language in the Workplace.* New York: Penguin Books, 1994.

Fisher, Roger, and William Ury. *Getting to Yes: Negotiating Agreement Without Giving In.* New York: Penguin Books, 1981.

Goldberg, Beverly. "Hi-tech Anxiety." *Management Review,* American Management Association. February 1998, 33–37.

Greenberg, Eric Rolfe. "Downsizing and the Career Path." *HR Focus,* American Management Association. March 1998, 2.

Kleinman, Carol. "Fewer Executives Being Promoted from Within." *The News-Times Business, Chicago Tribune on America Online,* May 5, 1998.

Mitchell, Frank, and Willis, Wes. *Relax and Live.* Audiotape component of *The Next Step: A Road Map to Recovery.* Manhattan Beach, CA: Dovetail Partners, Inc., 1997.

Sheehan, Daniel. *The Anxiety Disease.* New York: Bantam Books, 1986.

Smith, Adam. *Beyond the Backlash.* Public Broadcasting System, April 11, 1996.

Woititz, Janet. *Home Away from Home.* Pompano Beach, FL: Health Communications, 1987.

Index